Get to Work
Tucker Stein & Jack Osborn

Copyright © 2015
Tucker J. Stein
Jack L. Osborn

ISBN-13: 978-0692525388 (Career Success Press)
ISBN-10: 0692525386

About the authors:
 Get to Work is authored by Tucker Stein and Jack Osborn. After graduating the University of Redlands in 2011 with a Bachelor of Science in Business Administration and a minor in Economics, Tucker took a position with a Fortune 50 corporation in their management development program. Tucker has worked in London, New York City, Washington DC, Los Angeles and the San Francisco Bay Area, where he currently resides. Tucker is currently pursuing his Masters in Business Administration at the Stanford Graduate School of Business. He actively speaks at universities on career search and interviewing strategies and mentors students from his alma mater by helping with interview preparation and early career guidance. Tucker played NCAA football and remains an avid college sports fan.
 Jack Osborn holds the Hunsaker Chair of Management at the University of Redlands, and he is an alumnus with a degree in International Relations, graduating cum laude in 1969. He holds law degrees from the University of Edinburgh and Cambridge University in the United Kingdom. Jack has held senior positions with U.S. and foreign Fortune 100 corporations, and has worked in a variety of industries from food processing to high technology, including microelectronics, retail and traditional manufacturing, and federal government service. He has served as a Foreign Service Officer for the U.S. Department of State as the attaché for High Technology in Tokyo, Japan and as an analyst

for the U.S. Department of Commerce. He has managed business operations, sales, manufacturing and product development on four continents and has led acquisition teams in the United States and Western Europe. Jack advises his students seeking internships or career-path employment and his students have found both internships and career-path opportunities with a host of major corporations, both foreign and domestic. He also serves as the J.W. Fulbright Program Advisor for the University, in which capacity he has had the privilege of mentoring 20 Fulbright award recipients since 2008.

Recommendations:

In today's competitive job market, an edge is a necessity and the differentiator to kick starting a successful career; the work of Jack Osborn and Tucker Stein provides students this very advantage. In my personal experience, Jack's knowhow opened doors to outside academic opportunities that were critical to building my resume as an undergraduate. Tucker offered a unique perspective of the evolving job market and provided interview techniques applicable to all types of industries. The ability to work with Jack and Tucker gave me an unparalleled advantage in my job search, leading to offers from a variety of major corporations.

Mike
Financial Analyst, Fortune 30 Diversified Manufacturer

After being exposed to my work both inside and outside of the classroom, Professor Osborn saw a talent in me that I didn't necessarily see in myself. Alone, I would have never pursued a career opportunity in the industry and profession in which I now work. Because of the relationship with and guidance from Professor Osborn, I have been with that same employer for 13 years, in an industry that I'm passionate about and am achieving my goals in a profession for which I am truly well-suited.

Damon
Manager, Five Star-rated Commercial Insurance Company

Throughout my senior year, Jack mentored me in my career search, guided me as I evaluated job opportunities and potential career paths and spent countless hours coaching me to network, stretching me to excel in the classroom and developing my interviewing abilities. Leveraging Jack's connections and with his support, I was able to launch a successful career with a great company. Since my graduation, over the past 12 years, we have worked together as partners in building a talent pipeline for my company. By tapping into alumni, like me, that he developed, he has built a contingent of world-class graduate leaders invested in the success of our students.

Sara
Manager, Fortune 50 Retailer

When I first started at University, I was unaware of the opportunities that existed for young college graduates. Once I met Jack and took his first class, he showed me the importance of building a "story," not just a resume. We began working closely on my career path during my sophomore year, and although I was not sure of the career I wanted early in my college career, working with Jack put me on a path for success as an upperclassman. The preparation provided by Jack, and the lessons now referenced in this text, gave me the confidence I needed to perform during my final interviews.

Mackenzie
Analyst, Top-rated Financial Services Company

Overview:

Get to Work is primarily focused on two audiences. First, the text is directed at first-year students and sophomores to assist them in understanding how their entire college experience can be a career-building process. Second, *Get to Work* seeks to assist college juniors and seniors who are either searching for meaningful internships or who are seeking full-time positions after graduation.

This book is of great value to students pursuing a four-year college degree. It is of equal value to anyone who seeks to advise such students, be they professors, career guidance counselors, college administrators or parents. Additionally, it is designed to help Greek organizations and on-campus clubs that may seek to understand better how to support their members. Many potential advisors and counselors who may not have personal experience with job searches outside the realm of academia, or who may themselves not have graduated from college, can use this guide to assist students in the career-search process.

Get to Work is designed for students trying to understand how to build a strong undergraduate resume during the course of their studies and how to achieve maximum success in both internships during their junior or senior year and job searches during the senior year. It is important to note that job searches, once one has graduated and has a few years of work experience, will take on a very different format than you will find in this book. Whether you are a freshman building your resume for a first internship, or a senior accounting student seeking to work for a "Big Four" firm, this book will help you through the process and give you insight into every step on the journey to finding meaningful employment.

Scope of the text:

Get to Work is partly interactive and partly anecdotal. It is intended to provide the student, whether an experienced job seeker or a complete novice, with checklists, examples and guidance through a step-by-step process intended to maximize the possibility of attaining gainful professional employment. The task of preparing yourself to find the best internship or the best post-graduation job may appear daunting, and *Get to Work* is intended to provide clear and actionable help to students in all phases of the process, including networking, resume-building, interviewing and structuring your search for the right job.

We designed this book to be applicable to the internship and job search process for all majors. While many of the lessons, techniques and stories are best applied to those seeking business-related positions within companies of all sizes, we also offer advice on finding opportunities with service organizations and at all levels of government. If you are a S.T.E.M. major, we believe you can use our guidance to your advantage in your search for even the most technical positions.

Throughout the book, we provide dozens of "Insider Tips" and "Notes" which are real examples from many students whom we have coached through this process. We believe these insider examples will help you understand real-world job search situations and that you will be able to apply these lessons to your own search.

Inspiration for *Get to Work*:

Tucker and Jack were inspired to work together after realizing that Tucker and his classmates had struggled their way through the transition from student to employee without structure or a clear strategy. Today there is an array of career-search books written by human resource executives and industry professionals designed for those who have already commenced and established a career, already know their industries of interest and have an existing network of contacts. However, there is a dearth of resources designed specifically for college students.

Jack Osborn, who came from a series of executive global industry positions and has been working with college students for the past fourteen years, saw that while the students he personally coached were able to attain coveted positions with many Fortune 500 companies, there was a need for a roadmap that many more students could utilize. In the course of presenting job-search techniques to classes of university seniors the two men found many students asking the same practical, fundamental questions regarding the process.

This book answers those questions. This manuscript was created to help both those students who have a defined career target, and those who do not yet have a clear picture of the industry in which they would like to work. Those without direct work experience or a network to leverage will find the material valuable. College students juggle many things, and are often working to cover expenses, playing sports, serving in student government, pursuing academics and undertaking community service, not to mention enjoying an active social life. The time-constrained student overwhelmed by the daunting process of searching for an internship or post-graduation employment can use this tool to streamline their search, find efficiencies in the process and increase their return on invested time.

Acknowledgements:

Many thanks go to all the individuals who helped us with this work and who provided guidance and commentary through the process and to those who shared their stories with us, but who remain anonymous. Thanks go to Heather Thayer, Matt Dale, Thomas Hartwig, Christopher Kinney, and Wyatt Hanson for reading the manuscript, giving up considerable time and commenting on all aspects of the content. Particular thanks go to Matt Dale for his invaluable suggestions as to the ordering of the major components. Thanks to go to David Armstrong, Rachel Smith, Kara Babb, Mike Caston, Damon Morris, Kyle Proctor and Sara Bonino for their comments and insights. Beyond all this, thanks go to Kathy Osborn for her patience and support throughout the process, as without her support Jack would never have been able to contribute to the environment that led to many of the positive stories in this work. Additionally, thanks to Keith and Carol Stein for providing Tucker the opportunity to attend the University of Redlands, and for supporting him on his path since graduation.

Without the inspiration of role models like Jim and Althea Schroeder, Dan and Durene Hanson, Rich and Ginnie Hunsaker, Chuck Wilke, Cal Boothby, Lisa Swanson, Kim Stafford, Ron Gravette, Gary Byrne, Rob Harris, Scott Smith, Andrew Smaltz, David Maupin, and Donald Kohler, we would never have been able to create the very positive environment here at the University of Redlands which led to us being able to articulate and illustrate the importance of all the steps we have described in this process. Our friends and colleagues at the University have been a huge help in supporting our business students in both their educations and their career path efforts, including Chris Walker, Walter Hutchens, Mara‾ Winick, Jill Robinson, Graeme Auton, Bill Southworth and Barbara Pflanz. Our editor, Robin Stevens, has been very patient with us and has done much to improve the clarity of our expression. The friendship of Bob and Doreen Jackson, who have published so many important political and international works, has been a very special inspiration to this effort. Their focus and diligence in developing unique perspectives on complex problems is an inspiration to all whom have read their works. Finally, Jerry Baldwin and Jim Reynolds did much to provide a clear view of what recruiting and selecting talent is all about.

Disclaimer:

Please recognize that this work is the opinion of the authors and they reserve all copyright of the material. Do not solely rely on this text without seeking advice from career placement officers, your professors or other sources of credible information.

The structure of our book:
Get to Work is divided into five major sections as follows:

- Overview and inspiration
- Section I: The Freshman and Sophomore's Guide (17-68)
- Section II: The Preparation (69-119)
- Section III: The Application (120-128)
- Section IV: The Interview (129-188)
- Section V: Post Offer (189-208)
- Abridged Action Summary (209-214)

In Section I, "The Freshman & Sophomore's Guide," we highlight the importance of building a foundation for your portfolio early in your college career. We provide practical methods of planning your undergraduate experiences so you will be in the best possible position to point to your accomplishments when looking for an internship or job. This section acknowledges that along the way you may change your academic focus and career goals, even more than once, but that the meaningful experiences you gain outside the classroom can serve you on more than one path. Believe it or not, resume building starts the moment you set foot on campus! Please note that third and fourth year students will find great value in section I and we highly recommend that readers approach the text chronologically.

Section I includes the following subsections overviewed below:

- **How to build your resume** and decide what to include and what not to include. We placed resume building early in the materials because we want to show how critical the many aspects of your college life can be to telling your story. We will dive deep into key sections and specific terminology to include on your resume for success in the application process.

- **The role of internships** and why it is absolutely critical to have these types of experiences as an undergraduate. Companies, governments and not-for-profits look for students with real experience. Internships, particularly in your junior year and the summer between your junior and senior year, are critical for landing positions at major corporations. The paid internships offered by most Fortune 500 companies, and many others, afford students the opportunity to be exposed to one or more functions within a corporation during a summer or academic term. (Note: throughout the text we will use "Fortune" as a reference to Fortune Magazine's list of the largest companies by revenue. Fortune is a premier business publication in the United States.) At major corporations, internships are structured to ensure that you learn about the company and its business model and practices. These internships become a major talking point on your resume and are an area where interviewers will focus. We will closely examine the qualities companies are seeking in an intern, and how to best position yourself to earn these positions.

- **The importance of networking**, both for internships and for senior year post-graduation employment searches. Networking is the art of developing advisors, mentors and contacts who will help guide you to meaningful opportunities. Some will do this by sharing their own experiences, which can be incredibly valuable. Others may refer you to a friend or business associate who may or may not have an opportunity immediately awaiting, but who would be willing to speak with you, and help you out if there is a "fit." Networking is one of the hardest parts of the process for many students to undertake. Some feel it is in some way "improper" to discuss employment goals with family and friends - nothing could be further from the truth. We explain how to tactfully gain opportunities and advice from the people you know, be they coaches, friends, family, professors or administrators.

Section II outlines the key steps in the pre-application period. The text dives deep into typical timelines in the job search process, from understanding your strengths, weaknesses and interests, to building a list of target employers, to planning goals for your first few years of employment. We discuss how to stay organized in your search and we outline other administrative tactics to optimize your applications. Section II is critical to position yourself for success in the process.

Section III focuses on the nuances of the application and the position description. We examine how to thoroughly read a job description and how to organize and structure your application for the greatest success. We outline what to look for in every section of the job description and how to help your resume pass through the first round of screening. Many students fail to thoroughly understand the job description; we will highlight the key components and explain how to use them to win you an interview.

Section IV prepares students for the interview. The section outlines the many ways you should go about preparing for your interviews for both internships and full-time jobs, and walks through the steps that are required to succeed in each. This is another area where far too many students simply do not grasp the importance of extensive and thorough preparation. You are competing against the top students, from the Ivy League to top state universities and liberal arts colleges. You have to be ready and we give you an outline of how to do this.

We outline the different types of interviews and explain how to carefully structure your answers to position you for success. The interview often has different stages, first over the phone and as the process progresses, face to face. All types of interviews are fraught with their own challenges, which we will carefully outline. As hard as it may be to believe, interviewers, particularly if you progress to face-to-face interviews, are looking for reasons to disqualify applicants. We address the complexities of the interview process and provide you with winning approaches. We focus on how to open and close an interview, and share over fifty interview questions common to a variety of industries.

Section V outlines the required actions after the interview. The section walks through the different evaluation techniques and identifies next steps to either continue your search, or accept an offer. In this section we outline key aspects of offer evaluation, including the different components of the salary package. Many believe the process is winding down once the interview is completed, but some important steps are just beginning!

Section I: The Freshman and Sophomore's Guide

Our first section focuses on building the foundation for your resume, which will ultimately position you for both internships and full-time job offers. Please note that many of the subchapters are applicable to upper classmen, not just freshmen and sophomores.

Preparing yourself for post-graduate employment is a four-year journey

You begin building your resume in your first semester:
Positioning yourself for meaningful employment after graduation is a four-year journey that should **start in your first semester**. As soon as you step on campus, your high school days are over, and by the time you are a junior you can no longer use those earlier accomplishments on your resume. **Everyone interviewing you will look for what you have done in your college years -- high school is in the distant past and is now irrelevant.**

As you start your college tenure you must start thinking early **how to differentiate yourself** from your peers with the same majors and on-campus opportunities. For most full-time positions, there will be hundreds, if not thousands, of applicants! Annually we see a major commercial electronics company process 7,500 seniors and graduates for seven positions. Similarly, a major aerospace company interviews over one thousand candidates for ten coveted spots. But don't be discouraged, as you can make it all the way to a job offer, just as our students have done. To maximize the probability that you will be competitive for these positions, you need to start prepping the moment you come on campus. The building of your resume starts the day you arrive on campus and will continue throughout your entire undergraduate career.

Note: As an undergrad seeking internships, it's important to remember that you won't have many years of industry experience and the **companies understand this**. However, the interviewers, human resources representatives and managers know that throughout your time at university, you are afforded a unique opportunity to build leadership abilities and applicable skill-sets while, most importantly, learning how to think, reason and solve problems. Any potential employer will want to see that you've taken every available opportunity to prepare you for a position with their company.

The importance of the freshman year:
In your first semester, your concentration is, as it should be, focused on transitioning into college and finding your major or area of academic concentration. As you begin your second semester, you should start thinking about **positioning yourself** on a path for employment. From our experience, the students who have the most trouble in their

career search are those who wait until their junior or senior year before starting to consider meaningful academic coursework, work experiences and club involvements for their resumes. Your time at university affords you an uncommon environment perfectly suited for building your resume. Most universities have a plethora of clubs, organizations, or student government activities that provide you with paths to get involved in different learning and leading experiences. Use them.

Monitor your online presence:
Be aware that recruiters for both internships and full-time positions will review your online profiles for most social networking sites. Prepare for this early and monitor what is associated with your name online. Avoid any unprofessional photos and keep all your profiles on the highest privacy settings. Later we will touch on the specifics of background checks but saw it important to note this early.

Establish your mentors early:
When entering university it is easy to get lost in coursework and the bustle of college life while forgetting to establish mentors or advocates. A mentor, typically a professor, has the ability to see the opportunities (both at the university and beyond) from a broader perspective and with a keener eye, as they have seen students of previous classes and know what level and type of involvement typically results in full-time job offers. When entering university, try to find mentors that align with your interests and long-term goals. If

you're a business student interested in aviation, you may find someone within the engineering school or business department with relatable industry experience. More likely than not, these professors will enjoy speaking with a student taking specific interest in their field of study and will be eager to help you on your journey.

Mentors can provide real world experiences:

Professors are often agents for creating internship or on-campus case study opportunities. Many professors are searching for sharp undergraduates to assist them with some aspect of their research not already being handled by graduate students. Especially at colleges without extensive graduate programs, professors are often quite willing to take on one or two of the best and the brightest from the undergraduate student body (we will discuss key on-campus jobs in-depth later in this section).

Sometimes, at larger universities, professors are not as easily available. If this is the case, visit the development or career services offices to explore opportunities on campus. If you have a particular interest in a subject of one of the department's professors, reach out to explain your interest and request a short meeting to discuss the professor's focus. You will be surprised that many professors, lecturers, readers and teacher's assistants will be more than willing to speak with you about your shared interests.

Many universities offer real-world experience which pairs students with local businesses. This introduces them to hiring managers and exposes them to corporate work through company-sponsored case studies, or service projects helping to solve problems that a specific company or not-for-profit may be encountering. These experiences are invaluable for students when they begin the process of applying to companies for both full-time positions and internships.

Insider tip: You never know when someone may choose to think of you as a possible candidate. Remember, professors and other faculty and staff are often connected with outside activities. One talented student established a positive relationship with the Chair of International Relations. One day he walked into the office, and, quite unexpectedly, the professor looked at him and asked if he would be interested in participating in a political campaign experience. Six months later that student was working as a paid intern for one of the most powerful political campaigns in America.

Outlining your strengths, weaknesses and interests as a first step:
Considering you have limited experience and likely don't have a true understanding of an exact career path, there are some basic questions and exercises to consider when starting your collegiate career. It's best to start with the **fundamental understanding of your strengths, weaknesses and interests**. We recognize that your interests will change through college, but it is important to establish

general industries or functions of interest early in your collegiate career.

We recommend that you create the lists shown below, every semester, to track how your interests evolve over your college tenure.

You may not be quite sure how to describe your strengths, weaknesses and interests, so we have put together lists for each one on which you may find items that describe you. These lists are not all-inclusive and you should add to them as you see fit.

Strengths:

Weaknesses:

Interests:

Example Strengths: Small-group leadership; team player; good listener; analytic; strong writer; strong quantitative skills; aptitude for foreign languages; tenacity and energy; quick study; entrepreneurial; strong at multi-tasking; strong salesperson; get along well with my professors; respected by peers; dedicated to my assignments.

Example Weaknesses: Unaccustomed to public speaking; not quantitative; lack of technical skills; don't yet have a focused interest; easily flustered; not comfortable leading teams; not an analytic type; have difficulty keeping up with my course work; no work experience.

Example Interests (Be as specific as possible): Sports; service to others; specific clubs; church; dance, orchestra; reading; journalism; radio broadcasting, theater; managing others; leading teams; etc. **Industries** such as: Technology, Consumer, Healthcare, Aviation; **Skill-sets** such as: financial analysis, sales, marketing, writing.

Creating advantages through classes, clubs and organizations

A key step in finding an internship or full-time job is creating *leverage* through your undergraduate experiences. What we mean by leverage is the way you assess the experiences you have had, (internships, sports, school, service, etc.), and interpret them in ways both applicable to and desirable for the position you want.

In short, the goal of your undergraduate studies is to put yourself in a position to **take opportunities as they arise**. As a freshman or sophomore, you need to perform well in the classroom and develop a solid GPA base so that professors present you with opportunities to further your career goals. In the next few sections, we will discuss opportunities to create leverage in your first years and walk you through the main categories to consider as you build a strong transcript.

Classes:

Once you've identified your main strengths, weaknesses and interests, you can find classes that will complement your strengths, address your weaknesses and move you toward your long-term goals. College classes are the perfect place to gain in-depth knowledge and understanding of a subject. After completing the required courses, you have a significant amount of flexibility in choosing classes to meet certain other requirements and schedules. If you are able to add specialization through specific programs such as brand management, financial economics or human resources management, it will be an asset to your application. We recommend you select classes with an eye toward leveraging these units into an industry of interest.

In your first year, you should select the course schedule to give you the strongest foundation for your focus as an upperclassman. If there are classes that (either directly or indirectly) align with your interests, you should enroll. Additionally, it is encouraged to **take classes outside of your major** that may grant you exposure into an industry of interest. For example, if you're interested in the business of Renewable Energy, try to take an Energy Systems class within the science department, or a relevant course in Environmental Sciences. If some courses are closed to you because of required prerequisites you may be able to audit the course either officially or unofficially.

What are the "must-have" courses before your senior year?

Quantitative Coursework: Whatever field interests you, be it public relations, marketing or manufacturing, you cannot escape the need for math! Interviewers will pay particular attention to the quantitative coursework listed on your transcript. Whether you're applying for a quantitative position or not, companies will want you to have a good mathematical base. Be sure to integrate quantitative classes into your schedule early and, if possible, take Calculus I. If applying for a position in finance, accounting, banking or consulting they will likely dismiss an applicant for the lack of Calculus I on the transcript.

Language Coursework: In today's global marketplace, companies favor candidates who can communicate in a second language at least at an intermediate level. While many of their seasoned veterans have missed their opportunity to learn another language, your time at university provides you the perfect opportunity to develop second-language skills. **Note:** to be able to put a language on your resume, you will need **intermediate proficiency at a minimum**. As you advance in your language you may find that there are special courses offered that pertain to business. Believe it or not, there are a number of foreign language programs that offer training in how to communicate in that language using email (e.g. Mandarin Chinese)! Even if you are not a business major or minor, we encourage you to include such courses in your portfolio.

Demonstrating that you have second-language skills also proves to the interview team that you are a fast learner and may have an aptitude to work with international customers or teams.

Note: While Tucker was able to add specific technical coursework to his resume, his lack of second-language skills were a weak point. In several interviews Tucker was asked about his lack of a second language. If you don't have any second-language proficiencies on your resume, you will need to compensate in other areas of proficiency (i.e. quantitative).

Professional Writing: Companies are looking for new hires who can write in a professional capacity. Through conversational situations (i.e. email) and more formal circumstances (i.e. documents, letters to customers, assignment briefs), companies will evaluate you on your ability to write professionally. If such classes are offered, it is recommended to take a professional writing course prior to graduation and keep your writing skills sharp through coursework and papers.

Insider tip: Writing matters in all types of industries. A one billion-dollar in annual sales transportation company we know has finalists come in for a day of observation at one of their major yards. At the end of the day, finalists are asked to send in their written evaluation of the day's experience, capturing what they saw and learned. We had a call from the human resources representative, who explained that an otherwise highly-qualified candidate was not selected because he had failed the writing portion of the company's evaluation. Top firms from many industrial sectors will often ask you to provide a research and writing sample. Writing clearly and concisely matters whether you are going into retail, banking, manufacturing or logistics.

Public Speaking: If your institution offers public speaking courses, as many do, you need to take one. Some offer very specific courses, e.g. business speech, which is designed to assist you in understanding how to make a "no-notes" stand-up presentation and how to make a formal Power Point presentation. Students have shared that these courses are invaluable in developing their speaking skills and building their self-confidence. Clearly, students who are involved with mock court or debate have a leg up in this category, but everyone can attain acceptable speaking skills if they pursue the right opportunities.

You might say, "But my schedule is loaded and I don't have time to take another class." Across the nation there are opportunities through a national organization, Toastmasters, and there are also speech-training classes, such as the Dale Carnegie Institute, which focus on confidence building, mental organization and public speaking.

***Study Abroad opportunities*:** Employers favor students with study abroad experience. There are a number of reasons study abroad experiences are an asset to your resume. Fundamentally, employers will see this as you taking an opportunity to leave your comfort zone and try something new.

Studying abroad will reflect particularly favorably on your application if you have lived in a foreign-language speaking country and especially if you've lived with a host family away from other English speakers. Employers look for **well-rounded** recent graduates. Your ability to demonstrate that you've taken risks and are open to challenging experiences will be an advantage. Living abroad also shows employers that you have chosen to expose yourself to cultural diversity, a critical element in many hiring decisions.

An additional bonus will be any work experience you have had while studying abroad. If you are able to fit in an internship in another country it will show your determination and seriousness. Demonstrating that you have taken on additional challenges while living in a foreign country will be a major asset to your application.

The advantage of a business minor:
Many students may love history, biology, literature or dance, but most professions require some knowledge of business. We have seen biology students with terrific MCATs use the business minor to their advantage. Top medical school admissions offices

communicated to these students that it was their business minor that differentiated them from other candidates. Even if you are not studying business or finance in your major, consider minoring in one of these areas.

Differentiating yourself through your coursework:

When applying for an internship, organizations understand that you most likely don't have any past corporate experience, and **they don't expect you to**. Therefore, their requirements focus on GPA, relevant coursework, campus leadership, community service and extracurricular activities.

Explaining your double major (and minors):

If you were a double major, highlight it in your application and interview. Explaining to the interview team that you were a double major shows them that you often go above and beyond requirements, are a good worker and were able to foresee a potential intersection between your two fields of interest. Be prepared to articulate this intersection in your interviews, as you will be asked. Be sure to highlight any educational areas where you clearly excelled when compared to your peers.

Note: Tucker was extremely interested in finding a position with a solar cell manufacturer. With his strictly business and finance background he didn't have much experience in the required technical fields. Leading up to the summer of his junior year, Tucker added a class in renewable energies through the

29

science department. Taking this class afforded him not only a practical introduction to the technical aspects but also gave him the ability to demonstrate to his desired employer that his interest in their field had led him **beyond his specific course requirements to develop an understanding of the technical side of their operations**. With his new basic knowledge of solar energy, Tucker was differentiated himself from the majority of others applying for an entry-level finance position. When applying for an internship, your selected coursework makes it possible to stand out from other candidates.

On-campus clubs:

As an undergrad, on-campus clubs are excellent forums to explore industries of interest and gain leadership experiences. Clubs such as Rotaract or investment clubs can provide leadership experiences and specific technical skills for the job market. Rotaract is primarily the college arm of Rotary International, a major service organization that works on a broad array of projects from the local level to the international. Campus investment clubs are usually open to students of all majors, and sometimes manage a portion of their university's portfolio.

Clubs allow you to learn more about your interests through focused learning and hands-on activity. To build leadership experiences and to develop your network for internship opportunities, get involved early with industry-related clubs. To find the availability of these clubs visit your student center or the Clubs and Activities department.

Note: If there isn't a club for something that you're specifically interested in, it could be valuable to start and become the founding president of a club directly related to your interests and potential career path. Many departments will support you in starting a club. Holding a major role in an organization or creating an entirely new organization tells interviewers a great deal about your initiative and leadership.

Club Leadership:

Many students list clubs or other groups with which they have been involved, but just "being there" isn't enough. Joining for the sake of "hanging out" doesn't help in your internship and career search. What companies and their interviewers are looking for is not just the fact that you were a member of student government or a campus investment club. They want to know what you did and that you can demonstrate hands-on leadership.

For example, you want to be able to tell your interviewer that while attending Club X you were elected the Treasurer, or other cabinet position. But even that won't be enough. You want to explain that you did something truly innovative or audacious while serving as Treasurer. You overhauled the bookkeeping system and took the club from three semesters of being in the red to a point where it was on solid ground with sufficient funding. It definitely isn't enough to simply be a member; you need to be much more than that for your resume and personal story to really "pop" for the reader or interviewer. Remember, thousands upon thousands of students are involved with Greek Life or Student Government - **what did you do** that really made a difference? No one is impressed with the fact that you were a member, what they care about is what you did as a member, and they want you to be very specific.

Varsity sports, orchestras and jazz bands:
Involvement in varsity sports and organized music is highly sought after. Why? Because this involvement demonstrates one of the highest levels of teamwork, commitment and the ability to be coached. Many of you will have examples of team leadership. At the same time, carrying on varsity sports or musical involvement require considerable discipline and excellent time management skills. While this shouldn't be a main focus of your resume, it can be very helpful to have a bullet or two highlighting your athletic or musical involvement.

Community service:
Recruiters look for a well-rounded resume of someone who takes **every opportunity available to them**. Community service and not-for-profit based work is a great way to expand your resume. Most universities have a diverse range of not-for-profit and volunteer opportunities, which may be the perfect place to establish your niche or develop a focus. Recruiters look for candidates who are **unique** among their classmates and can tell a story through their resume. If you're able to leverage

these volunteer activities into your personal story, you greatly increase your odds of earning an interview.

Greek organizations:

There has been so much negative publicity surrounding fraternities and sororities that we don't recommend you reference a mere membership in one. If you have held an elected office and actually done something while holding the office, then it is fine to reference and explain your involvement. We suggest that you refer to your fraternity or sorority as a "Greek organization" and spell out the identifying Greek letters. When describing your organization, list some of the principles that the organization was founded upon, for example: Delta Gamma; founded on teamwork, leadership and service.

There are also some organizations that are service, academic honors or education organizations first, and social organizations second, and it is fine to indicate your involvement with these entities. An example of this type of organization would be Delta Sigma Pi, a national Business and Economics Greek organization that stresses the business education of its members. While Delta Sigma Pi does have a social aspect, the fraternity was formed for the education of its members in regards to business types and practices.

Is the organization national?

Is the group you're joining a national organization? If so, it may provide very good networking opportunities. By national, we mean an organization that has a presence on many campuses across the nation. Some colleges only have local Greek organizations. In that case, the networking aspects are somewhat limited. But if you are working with a national organization, whether it is a social organization such a Greek fraternity or sorority, or a service-type body such as Rotaract, (which is present on many college campuses and which, as noted, is the college arm of Rotary International) you have the opportunity to network with leaders across the nation. Many students attend regional or national conferences as part of their active memberships, which brings excellent networking opportunities. National clubs in your town, such as Rotary, Kiwanis or The Optimists, and many other civic organizations consist of local business people, educators and city government employees. Retired executives populate many Rotary clubs and provide great mentors and contacts.

On-campus jobs:

On-campus tutoring or teaching assistant positions allow you to demonstrate classroom leadership and above-average proficiency in a subject. Typically, each department has positions to tutor peers while receiving work-study credits or payment. Exploring opportunities to tutor may bring you closer to the professors in your department and provide a valuable resume line item in the "Education" section. If you are looking to go into sales, the development office is a great place to work during the school year, as it affords you the opportunity to be involved in solicitations of both alumni and friends of the university.

Building your Resume

Your resume can be your most valuable asset or your greatest liability in landing your first job. Once submitted, it is final and thus it must be carefully structured and reviewed again and again. In this section we outline how to properly build your resume. Though we will go into further detail in the subsequent pages, the general outline for your resume should be as follows:

- **Centered Header:** Include your name and all contact information (be sure to triple-check that your contact information is correct – incorrect contact details can have drastic results!)
- **Education & Awards:** University and major, anticipated graduation date, GPA and relevant coursework. Include any study abroad experiences. If you are proficient in a foreign language, include it here. If you received a scholarship to attend university, you should indicate the name of the award in this section.
- **Varsity Sports, Music, Student Government:** Each of these should be enumerated. List the position or instrument played and the length of time. List any major honors achieved, either individually or team-based.
- **Work experience:** Any relevant internships, on-campus positions or

summer employment. Include 4-5 bullet points outlining your responsibility in each role.

- **Volunteer work or extracurriculars:** Include any relevant volunteer work or extracurricular experiences. Include any membership in Greek organizations and offices held. List any on- or off-campus club involvement (particularly highlighting your leadership in any organizations).
- **Computer and technical proficiencies:** State your proficiency in any advanced training or knowledge in Excel or databasing. (If you are running short on space, this may be included in the extracurricular or honors section above).

A few rules for constructing your "work experience" bullets:

- Only list major accomplishments; no small actions or achievements
- Build a story with your resume! Don't just list "filler" activities
- Keep sentences short and powerful
- Keep consistency in tenses, grammar and sentence structure
- Avoid repeating words or phrases
- Lead sentences with active (not passive or collective) verbs (these will be discussed later in the section)

Dates matter:

All items on your resume should carry a date. When constructing the education and work experience sections, list the school accomplishments and positions reverse chronologically, with the most recent first.

Items to keep off your resume:
- Political parties and advocacy groups (unless you are applying to work for a politician)
  - Political campaign experience is fine, just avoid identifying yourself as a Democrat or Republican. It is perfectly fine to state that you worked for a "California senator." It is unnecessary to state who that politician was, or what party they are associated with. The risk is not that the organization will care, but that the personal opinion of the person reviewing your application might negatively effect your candidacy.
- Too many fraternity/sorority references (As explained above, Greek life references are OK, but use conservatively)
- Religious affiliations
- High school accomplishments (Unless unbelievably profound)
- Personal references
- Photos (We realize that some overseas cultures wish to have a photo, but it is not appropriate in applying for a position

with a U.S. company. Always check carefully before you include a photo.)
* Quotations
* Paper with vibrant colors

What does it mean to "Build a Story"?

With limited experience, as a soon-to-be graduate, it is important to demonstrate to your application reviewers how you've taken your experiences in the past four years to prepare yourself for the upcoming opportunities. Companies want to see how you've performed in your work or internship experience and what you can accomplish in a short amount of time. Building a story means to demonstrate how you've grown through your collective experiences. Have you gone from last to first in number of sales executed? Have you picked up skills outside of your classwork? What have you learned? Building a story is your opportunity to show growth and development through your limited experiences, and demonstrate that your history has prepared you for the desired job.

Should I have a resume objective?

Though the inclusion of a resume objective is up to personal preference, we recommend leaving it off. Your stated objective may appear either too broad or too narrow when reviewed by the human resources department. If you do choose to include an objective, be careful that its wording falls exactly in-line with the requisition descriptions for the job to which you are applying.

The "must-have" sections of your resume:

Headers and contact information:

It is important to have a clear header section of your resume with your name (centered) and all the following contact information:

- Full name
- Email address (be sure create a **Google Mail account**, rather than your university address which may be deleted after graduation)
- Home contact address
- Phone number

Keep the header simple and clear. State your name and contact information, nothing else. When listing your name, it is OK to list your middle initial or full middle name, but it is not necessary. Reminder: **double check** all the contact information as it is easy to include a typo.

Education:

Your education section should come immediately following the header. State your university and location, graduation date and major (and if applicable, minor) concentration. Be sure to highlight any double majors. Identify your degree as a Bachelor of Arts, or a Bachelor of Science. You may list both your cumulative and major GPA, but if you're only going to list one, list your **cumulative GPA**.

Though it is up to the preference of the applicant, some students prefer to list any relevant coursework. We recommend you consider listing key classes, particularly upper-level **quantitative coursework** if you are applying to any management or financial role. If you choose to do so, please keep the lists conservative (maximum five courses) and only list your most senior and advanced courses or honors projects. If you list awards or major projects, write a clear sentence stating the background of the work.

How do I demonstrate quantitative coursework?

Even if you do not have a minor in computer science or math, it is important to list a few applicable quantitative courses on your resume. Such classes may include: calculus, accounting, statistics and micro-economics. Employers of all industries and job types look for applicants with quantitative proficiencies.

Work Experience:

Typically students have **two to four** major positions to list in their experience section. The work experience section can include anything from your summer internship, your on-campus position leading a club or summer employment. Whatever you choose to include, these must be listed in **reverse chronological** order. Under each position, list three to four bullets reflecting only your major accomplishments or responsibilities from each position. Do not include clerical duties; if that is what you were doing, you should use a term such as "provided general office support." Highlight all leadership experiences and be sure to use action verbs, as explained below.

The importance of "I" versus "We":
   It is key to distinguish between participation and leadership. Many applicants will use words such as "worked," "joined" or "participated" when speaking about a project. Companies want those who have led projects or efforts. Though it is important to demonstrate that you are a good teammate, companies will be looking for leadership. The appropriate active verbs will reflect your impact.

Action verbs to use in constructing the story of your work experience:
- Led
- Organized
- Tracked
- Created
- Analyzed
- Coordinated
- Designed
- Consolidated
- Presented
- Performed
- Modeled
- Produced
- Instructed
- Scheduled
- Resolved

Your resume will be audited!
Recognize that what you put on your resume will be audited during the interview process. If you choose strong words like "led" or "managed," you can expect to be asked specific questions about what you actually did. Remember, interviewers are experienced and can easily tell if you are exaggerating. To avoid any disqualification or embarrassment, only include terms that you can explain carefully and fully. Another reason to be careful is that you may want to share your resume with professors or administrators, and it is very important that you not exaggerate your involvement with any organization.

Recently, one of our graduates interviewing with a major French company was immediately tested for his fluency in French and his intermediate competency in Portuguese; both of which were listed on his resume. Be aware that they will test your language skills if they are stated!

Community service & Extracurricular activities:
Human resources representatives and hiring managers will look to see what other organizations you're involved with outside of your classes. They will be interested to see if you've taken leadership positions with those clubs or community service groups. Community service is viewed as an asset and should be recognized on your resume. In general, keep this section brief but explain any

focuses that you've had through these opportunities. For example, if you've been involved in a student investment fund, bring this to attention for a finance-based application. If you have organized and led major charity fundraisers, interviewers want to see these types of management activities and will want to ask you questions about how big and how complex the activity was. Interviewers seek candidates with leadership experience and the extracurricular section is a fantastic opportunity to demonstrate these qualities.

Computer proficiencies:

At this point in your studies **it is expected** that you are proficient in the entire Microsoft Office suite. The most critical portion is your explanation of your level of proficiency with Excel. If not explicitly explained, interviewers will be keen to understand your literacy with the tool and may ask you to verbally work through a few Excel problems.

Beyond listing any advanced Excel knowledge, if you have a proficiency in something unique such as Salesforce or SQL, list it on your resume. Technical proficiencies are always an asset to your application, but everyone is expected to know the Microsoft Suite, so if that is all you have there is no need to list it. **Note:** One of the major questions Tucker struggled with during one of his final round interviews was regarding a step-by-step explanation of an Excel function. Be prepared for these types of questions.

Keep it to one page:
Keep in mind that reviewers expect no more than one page from an undergraduate student. You may feel that the one-page format looks a little crowded, but do not worry, unless you are applying for a position in graphic design, the interviewers are looking purely for the content information.

Career centers may have online software to help create your resume:
Check in with your career center to see if they provide resume-building software. This software typically helps track your college leadership experiences, key coursework and extracurricular involvement. There are a few different programs for resume building; the most common software products are: Resume Maker Pro and SelectSoft Resume Writer.

Summary:
Use your resume to tell the reader a story of how you've grown with your experiences and how you'll be able to apply these past experiences to the new position. Be straightforward and honest, and use action verbs. Highlight your strengths while also providing the reader with insight to your personality and interests. Always have your resume reviewed (many professors will be willing to help) and keep it clean and professional.

Internships

Internships are more than just a foot in the door. Internships provide students with opportunities to enhance their senior year job applications. First, they provide students with real-life working experience that can directly lead to full-time employment. Second, internships provide an opportunity to find your strengths and weaknesses, and to begin to understand your industry and organizational preferences. Third, internships provide an expanded network and the ability to say, "I've had a **similar experience** doing…" Internships will expose you to industries and functional roles, providing insight to what types of positions you will want to target for full-time employment.

Finding internships at small versus large companies:

Internships, particularly unpaid internships at smaller organizations, can be landed in a sometimes less formal approach as compared to a full-time offer. To find internships, your personal network can be the most powerful tool available. At smaller organizations, managers can sometimes justify hiring their friend's children as an unpaid intern much easier than they can justify providing someone with a full-time job. With this in mind, your direct network is often the highest probability for success in your internship search.

Similar to entry-level positions, there are different tactics in finding internships in large vs. small organizations. Within large organizations, there is a structured online application process similar to the process for full-time positions. The internship applicant goes through mostly the same level of screenings as entry-level positions. However, the requirements are more focused on GPA, coursework and extracurricular activities or club leadership, as they understand most students won't have previous work experiences in major organizations.

General timeline for internships:
     Many of the top brand names start their interview processes for summer internships between your junior and senior years as early as **September or October of your junior year**. Yes, companies start their interviewing processes seven months or more before the start date for their internships! This means that you have to be ready to get your applications submitted as soon as you return to school in the fall of your junior year. That said, some companies, primarily smaller organizations, will fill their internship slots beginning in the second semester. Be aware of the varying timelines and be sure to check online for requisition closure dates.
     Additionally, top companies will often take only a select group of rising juniors into their internship classes. Underclassmen need to keep this in mind when building their list of target companies, as very few major corporations accept students who have not completed their junior year immediately prior to the internship. With that said, more and more

companies are beginning to reserve internship spots for highly qualified underclassmen.

Underrepresented minority internship opportunities:

There is a wide range of organizations seeking to promote the candidacy of minority students. One example is Inroads, which provides talented underserved students with mentor coaches who will help them prepare for interviews with the most appropriate corporation. INROADS has established relationships with some of the nation's leading corporations both for internships and for jobs at graduation.

Another example is ALPFA, the Association of Latino Professionals For America. These organizations have led our students to programs where they have been flown across the country to participate in a case study competition sponsored by a "Big Four" accounting firm and a major aerospace manufacturer.

Will you be willing to work for free?

When beginning your internship search, you must decide: are you able to work for free if it comes to it? If so, the option of working for free will change your approach, allowing you to be more selective in your target companies. Offering to work for free can be a big asset in your application if you use it correctly, but don't play your cards too soon. If there is a company that exactly fits your interests and is seemingly perfect for an internship, first apply, and then later if it comes to earning the position or not, suggest that you would consider working for free or for a prorated salary. Don't lead with this offer as it may seem desperate. Most companies will clearly explain on their requisition if the internship is paid or unpaid, but it may be ambiguous in some smaller organizations.

Note: We have had students go "door to door" to companies that they have been interested in offering to work for free for a few days per week over the summer. These companies will likely be impressed by your tenacity and may allow you to join their team during your summer. Our students have held other paying summer jobs throughout the week, to balance a few days spent unpaid.

Internships expose you to all types of professionals and industries:
When Tucker was abroad in 2010 he worked for a financial services firm as a staff analyst. Aside from confirming for him that he wanted to work in financial services, it gave him leverage for other internships and full-time careers, (additionally it taught him that he wanted to work in a big city). That following summer, knowing that he wanted to work in financial services, he narrowed his search to all fields of financial services. Furthermore, Tucker narrowed his search exclusively to New York City. His strategy was that if he was not able to land an internship in finance, he was going to get as close to the financial district as possible to have the chance to meet people in the industry face-to-face. Internships provide

not only a base of understanding of what industry or role you want, but the ability to fact-find through your experiences and introductions. Ultimately, though Tucker was not offered any finance internships for the summer, he did find an intern marketing role that allowed him to network with his target finance companies.

Remember, as a recent graduate, figuring out what you **don't want to do** is just as important as finding what you **want to do**. In short, working in an organization allows you to gain real insight into yourself, which is much more valuable than any advice you can read on the Internet.

Internships force you outside of your comfort zone:

In his sophomore summer, Tucker took a position working for a major restaurant chain in their product development division. Though he knew nothing about promotional sales, he dove in with the goal to learn as much as possible. When hiring interns, human resources departments often look to past internship experience to see if you have at least some type of experience working in a similar setting or field. You may be surprised at the various ways you'll use the experience you acquire in your variety of roles.

Internships will teach you about industries, and work locations:

We have seen students take internships in selected business fields, such as retail or finance, and find that these industries are not for them. We've also seen students take internships in foreign countries, where they subsequently made the decision to change their personal language focus from Italian to Chinese, or vice versa. In even a short period, you may learn the valuable information that a previously desired role is not right for you. Luckily, your time spent within any organization will expose you to different departments and allow you to find roles more closely aligned with your developing goals.

Know what you want to accomplish as an intern:

If there isn't a formal, structured internship program, you should think carefully about what you want to accomplish, write down and organize a schedule, and share that with your mentor or the individual who is hiring you. They will appreciate that you are offering suggestions as to what you want to learn while on the job.

Some of the best internships are at major corporations:

If you are hired into an internship program with a national or regional brand, it is likely to be structured so that you will learn about the company while they learn about you. Such programs have briefings to which you will be invited and at which company management will share perspectives on the organization and what it is attempting to accomplish. You will be assigned a mentor or supervisor who will guide you through your daily tasks. Additionally, there will also be an educational-informational aspect to the internship, where you will have a chance to learn more about the company and the industry.

The value of a brand name:

Remember, a brand-name internship tells future interviewers that you were selected in a rigorous merit-based competition, with lots of applicants. Additionally, it isn't decisively important if that internship was in a different field from that of your final job search. In a perfect world, it is valuable to have a successful internship in the same industry as your job search, but it is not necessary. We know of a successful graduate who did their internships in retail analysis at a corporate headquarters, but chose an opportunity with a major investment bank. Brand names can help your resume stand out and help establish your credibility among other human resource departments.

Not a junior or senior? What do to with your summer?

Name brand internships are typically reserved for rising seniors. Before you find yourself eligible for a top internship, say in your first summer, try to find yourself a paid hourly retail opportunity with a major brand name company that exposes you to their business practices and monitors your sales progress. It is very valuable on your resume to quantitatively demonstrate your progress as a summer hire.

Insider Tip: In the summer before his senior year, Tucker applied to dozens of Fortune 100 internship programs but received zero Fortune 100 offers. With little luck at the major companies, Tucker refined his targets to smaller and mid-sized New York City-based companies. Tucker ended up in a terrific summer internship that was structured similarly to a program that you would see at a major corporation. Please keep in mind that if you aren't selected for an internship with a Fortune 100 you can still have a successful summer experience!

Are there limitations for foreign students?

If you are an undergraduate student holding an F-1 Visa, you should be able to apply for an internship. Read the U.S. Department of Immigration website carefully, as anything we are sharing with you here is merely advisory, and you should personally research all information pertaining to your situation. One important aspect to consider is that any time spent in an internship as an undergraduate will be deducted from the one optional grant that allows you to remain in the United States post-graduation for up to one year. Students who study specific subjects of interest to the United States government, e.g. mathematics, may be able to apply for an additional extension. But you must be able to demonstrate that you are using the allowed major in your work. This extension would allow you to remain in the United States and work for a company resident in the United States for an additional 17 months. Thus, in a perfect world, if you did not do an undergraduate internship in the United States, and you had an approved major such as math or biology, you might be able to stay and work for a total of 29 months after graduation. What does this mean? Because of the significant extension, during which time you are permitted to work full time, the option to apply for a permanent approved work status visa may present itself. To learn more about how students working under this program are handled in terms of applications for the F-1 OPT Visa, check out the U.S. Immigration website. Please note that major corporations will have someone within their human resource function who will be familiar with this program.

Networking Before the Application Submittal

Networking is an art that requires strategy, confidence, and most importantly, preparation. Networking is an opportunity to connect. To connect, you need to capture a person's interest by engaging in an intelligent conversation about the industry and their career. When you are going to meet with someone, whether it be a phone conversation with a professor's friend, or a meeting a family friend, you must ***make them comfortable with your personality and confident in your abilities***. Networking takes more than an amiable personality, it takes significant due diligence and preparation.

Utilizing your network's network:

The idea of "six degrees of separation," that in theory we are only six steps away from any other person, applies to networking yourself into an organization. In the competitive market today, many students unfortunately write themselves off after skimming through their list of contacts. When outlining your networking plan, consider whom you might be connected to outside of your immediate circle. When addressing your close contacts about your job search, indicate the industries you are following and explain that you're interested in talking with **anyone they might know**. The success of this approach can depend on your familiarity with your initial contact, and their belief that you're worthy of a recommendation.

Insider Tip: One very successful job seeker leveraged his personal relationships to identify a CEO at a Fortune 200 company, whose daughter was a friend. He asked the daughter if she would reintroduce him to her father, whom he had met a couple of times over the years. She was happy to do so and the student arranged a networking meeting with the CEO. After that meeting the CEO suggested to his senior human resources manager that the student be considered if any appropriate opportunities emerged. Today that job seeker manages a network of factories across Asia.

Know whom you'll be speaking with:
When given the opportunity to speak with someone who might be a strategic contact, use the chance to impress them with your due

diligence. Things to know about a point of contact before your meeting:

- Where they went to university and what they studied
- Where their career path has taken them (previous positions)
- Have they published in journals or written books? What is their main area of emphasis today?
- What were they doing at your age? Are there similarities in your paths?
- If possible, find out what they like to do in their free time; you might share interests
- Know their role within their organization and have a basic familiarity with the business and their products

Insider tip: People like to talk about themselves and they like to talk to people who have a genuine interest in what they do. Identify what you think is important to them and bring these interests into a conversation. Don't blatantly display all the information you know about the contact, but by tying their career or other public interests into the conversation, they will be able to tell that you have done your due diligence.

Insider tip: Don't be embarrassed to use your personal network. There is nothing wrong with going to your aunt who is in management or your father who is involved with sales and asking them about opportunities. Utilize your friends' families, too. One student talked to her older brother, who referred her to one of his favorite professors and she ended up with a great job with a national retailer. This was all because her brother's professor, from a completely different type of college, took action to help her find the best possible position and put her in touch with human resources managers at a company he knew well.

If you belong to a Greek organization, a varsity sports team, a symphony orchestra, debate society or jazz band, try to find out what the graduated members are doing and get in touch with them. Do not underestimate your contacts, or who they can put you in touch with – though you may not know it, your network's network is strong!

Use your local professional organizations:
At the end of his sophomore year, one of our students went through his local Chamber of Commerce directory and found an early-stage company that was working out of a garage. He ended up working for them forty hours per week unpaid, while working an evening restaurant job as a source of summer income. In this start-up company, our student held a number of roles, and earned direct experience working with customers. When he applied for junior year internships, he leveraged his start-up marketing and sales experience and got a very good paid marketing position with the world's largest food company. Today he is an account manager with that company in Northern California.

Networking yourself into a smaller organization:

Small organizations provide you with many avenues to find a specific contact within the organization. Under the "about" or "team" webpages you can find a list of managers and their functions. Your first step to navigating a smaller organization's job or internship requisition is to identify the hiring point of contact; often they will be listed as a human resources representative. Ideally, you will find someone titled "college recruiter." Next, identify a point of contact in the specific division or team you would like to join. For example, when Tucker was going through his search, he would find the sales manager or an analyst for a specific team of interest. To begin, *establish two points of contact.*

If you are lucky enough to get a response to your informational interview request, this is your time to impress. Be thoughtful about how you should approach speaking about your recent application. Ask questions about the individual, *ask intelligent questions about the industry*, but **don't** ask for a job because this person likely doesn't have the ability to hire and you don't want them to feel used or pressured. In closing the conversation, explain that you are in conversation with a recruiter or a human resources manager, and let them know how much you have learned from the discussion. Send a follow-up email thanking them for their time and reiterating how much you appreciate the opportunity. If you hold a good conversation, they may put in a good word for you with the human resources department.

Sometimes, recommendations come from the least likely of sources:

Hiring managers can be very helpful and will sometimes initiate further opportunities for you, even if they cannot place you themselves. Recently, we had a student with substantial abilities in computer science and working experience in high tech. While interning with a Silicon Valley tech company, the hiring manager was very impressed with the student and asked him to come back at the end of the day for a brief recap. In that meeting the manager shared that it would be almost impossible for him to hire the student, because he wasn't from the list of targeted schools (we will touch on target schools later). But the hiring manager promised to put the student applicant in touch with one of his colleagues at another similar company. The student was ultimately contacted, interviewed and spent his junior summer in a challenging internship in the Pacific Northwest.

Keep your network current and strong:

You must **follow up with your points of contact** and thank each person for his or her time. As they may speak to the hiring managers on your behalf, it is important for point of contacts to understand that you found their input valuable and that you plan to continue the relationship into the future.

Go have coffee!

One of the best ways to network is to arrange to have coffee with a point of contact. Coffee brings them out of their office, allowing them to more easily open up about their career and give thoughts on your application. Coffee is shorter than having lunch and can be scheduled at any time of the day. During your application period, challenge yourself to have coffee at least once a week with all different types of contacts.

Have your resume available:

Always be prepared to share your resume with the point of contact. Though it may be impossible to bring your resume to every meet and greet, be prepared to send them your resume during your meeting. Keep your resume stored in an email on your phone allowing you to quickly send if requested. Also, if some major new item is added to your resume you may want to share the updated version with your contacts. Be sure to include a note in the email body thanking them for their support and indicate that you have revised your resume to include a new award or new job.

Be prepared for the conversation:

What type of questions might you be asked? Prepare for where you believe the informational interview might go. Always have questions ready to fall back on if you reach an awkward point in the interview. When in doubt, **prepare**. An informational interview is no different in importance than a job interview and you must **prepare as if it was the final round**.

What do companies look for in an intern?

Companies understand that as an intern, you may not have experience working in a business prior to your internship. Knowing this, during an internship interview, the **questions largely revolve around your coursework and your on-campus experiences**:

What types of experiences are desired in an intern?

It is important to recognize that even for internships, companies look for experience. Retailers are looking for people who have sold a product and led small teams. Investment banks are looking for students with good quantitative skills who have possibly worked at a local brokerage office. Logistics and distribution companies are excited about students who have experience, even on campus, with organizing and managing small teams.

Communication matters:

When interviewing for an internship, companies focus primarily on your ability to articulate your relevant experiences. As internships often provide the company their first batch of candidates to hire as first year employees, companies look for someone who is both intelligent and would be a good fit with the company. Their assessment of your personality during the interview process will indicate "fit" with their culture. The internship gives them a trial period to test your work ethic, attitude and technical skills in the marketplace. Much of your time as an intern may be spent shadowing a few mentors. To add value in the short time you spend with the company it is imperative that you both listen and communicate well with your mentors and co-workers.

"GPA Means Everything" Fact or Fiction?

You have all heard, "GPA doesn't matter when you're in the workplace." We admit this is partially true. However, **GPA does matter** tremendously to get you *into* the workplace. Due to a huge number of applicants and a limited number of positions, **human resources professionals will often divide the number of resumes they need to read in half by removing all resumes below a certain GPA**. Additionally, early in your college career when you don't have the base of past marks from previous semesters, one poor grade can greatly drive your cumulative GPA downwards. It is important to keep this in mind and recognize that every class does matter and can possibly help or hinder your opportunity to get an internship.

You'll be competing against the maximums, not the minimums!

Companies will almost always include a minimum GPA requirement for their positions. For many competitive positions the requirement will be 3.5 and above, while other, less competitive positions may require a 3.2 cumulative GPA. Though you may make the minimum requirement, know that you will be **competing for a position against the maximums, not the minimums.** Ultimately, GPA does matter and can disqualify you from consideration for many positions.

Top financial firms are looking for a 3.7+ GPA, as are the leading high-tech companies. Retailers tend to work in a band of 3.0 to 3.3 as minimums. Most of the highly successful brand names are looking for a minimum of 3.5. If you don't have the grades, you need a very strong story of success in sports, student government or service to create a balance.

To secure a full-time position, you must perform!

If you perform well as an intern, you will likely be extended an opportunity to interview for an entry-level position. If the company takes on a set amount of new hires from each graduating class, they will earmark a number of interview spots for previous interns. If you are interning with a smaller organization, be sure to inquire about potential openings for the next summer and stay in touch with your internship mentors throughout the year. The hiring managers will always request input from your direct internship manager, which will likely be the focal point in any decision to extend you an offer.

If you go through an internship, apply to be a full-time hire and are not offered a position, you are unlikely to be extended an offer if you apply again. Internships are a 10- to 12-week evaluation period, and poor performance during this short time will eliminate you from future consideration.

The internship is truly an extended interview:

Many major corporate internships are designed to help companies to find the best and the brightest as early as possible in order to secure these high-achieving interns at the end of their internship. We have seen such offers in the aerospace, financial and retail industries, and there are many others. Managers, especially your direct supervisor or mentor, will be judging how you work with your peers, with your seniors and with people of diverse academic backgrounds and personality.

In an internship, you are never off the job. Don't post your opinions anywhere on the web. Don't think that because you are out only with other interns from the same company that your behavior won't get back to your supervisor or mentor. Be very careful not to criticize your company. Remember, an internship is an extended interview. But if you perform well, and fit in with the company culture, you could very well receive a formal job offer before even beginning your senior year! Also, remember that many HR professionals talk about candidates they may hire - a good, or bad impression with one may carry over to other companies.

What the company does and doesn't expect from an intern:

Being thrown into a ten-week internship is a crash course in how businesses operate. Most organizations **_don't_** expect you to come in and revolutionize the way that they do business. They do expect you to come in and have an understanding of how the department operates within their larger corporate structure.

At a minimum, you should start your internship already knowing:
- How does the company make money?
- How do they differentiate their product or service?
- How are they doing in the marketplace?
- How are their competitors doing within the marketplace? Are they gaining or losing market share and why?

What will you actually do as an intern?
Internships vary widely in terms of exposure to the workings of a company and its industry. Some internships include assigning the intern a project, in addition to their more routine duties. These assignments vary, but the student is usually asked to analyze some aspect of the organization and propose a program or solution that might assist the company, or the business unit in which they are stationed. Recently, we have seen students assigned to address workflow, and platforms for more effective department communications. Usually, at the end of the internship, the student is given an opportunity to present their research and suggestions to a management team. These types of projects are incredibly helpful in building your resume.

How well are interns paid?

As a generalization, with major corporations you can expect the salary range to be surprisingly broad, stretching from about $14 an hour to $25 an hour, with expectations that you will work a 40-hour week. Pay isn't the only compensation, however. If you are accepted into an internship in another city, say at a major corporate headquarters, check out in advance how the hiring company helps you with accommodations. Some companies even pay modest internship relocation stipends to help you get started at their offices. Some companies provide housing and even company shuttles, some provide advice and guidance regarding housing and even offer a service to connect interns prior to the start date. There are many variables regarding compensation for an internship, but it is important to find out in advance.

Inquire about a travel allowance!

Sometimes in dealing with a smaller corporation or a private firm you may be able to negotiate some sort of travel allowance, if you have to commute a considerable distance each day. Plan your negotiation carefully, and be prepared for the worst, but if the company has made you an offer and you know you will be driving 70 miles round-trip every day, it does not hurt to ask.

Post-graduate internships:

While the vast majority of companies will actually make a job offer and officially hire you out of university, there are a few very prominent companies that instead start out graduating seniors with an internship. Don't be shocked, as this is these companies' way of addressing the situation of possible poor performance while seeing if you are a good cultural fit, very early in your career. In other words, you will be hired technically as an intern, but after (usually) 90 days you will be reviewed, and if your performance has been strong, you will be hired as a full-time employee.

Though these internships may appear similar to those that many students secure during the summer before senior year, they are not. When you are searching for full-time employment, do not confuse the junior-year summer internships with the post-graduation internship opportunities. Usually the employer will clearly state what academic year, e.g. must have junior standing. If there is no clear academic standing listed, call the corporate human resources department to clarify. The key to these types of internships is being sure you know what happens at the end of the internship, before you start and getting it in writing. Find out the position to which you would be assigned, the location and the first-year salary, benefits and how frequently you will be reviewed. You need to be clear on what the post-internship position is before you sign up for the internship.

Section I Summary:
College is an investment. It is a time to grow your knowledge and position yourself for career success. With all the excitement and distractions it is easy to lose focus on aligning

yourself early to leave college with a platform to apply your interests and your strengths in a career. Be **willing and able** to challenge yourself and go out and find opportunities that make sense for you. Find mentors, develop your interests and build a skill set that allows you to tell a story to leverage into a full-time career upon graduation.

Structure of the third and fourth year student's Get to Work guide

In the following sections, though the references are pertaining to full-time jobs, the text contains lessons and techniques that can also be applied to the underclassman's internship search. Additionally, though many of our stories revolve around Fortune 500 companies, all the lessons and processes are applicable to companies of all sizes. In the past section we've gone over how to build your profile as an underclassman, and how to properly organize your resume. With these two fundamentals covered, we will now move to the full-time job-search process in the following order:

- Section II: The Preparation
- Section III: The Application
- Section IV: The Interview
- Section V: Post Offer
- Checklist for success: your footnotes in the process

If needed, please refer back to the prior
sections as you work through the text. Likewise,
if you'd like to skip ahead to certain sections,
this manual is designed to allow reader
flexibility.

Section II – The Preparation

Introduction:

There are a few fundamental steps in everyone's career search. In this section we will go over the first steps that will get you on your way to full-time employment. The primary steps are as follows:

1) Preparing for the typical milestones and timelines of the process
2) Knowing yourself, your interests, your strengths and how to leverage them in a career
3) Finding and targeting companies and industries that are in a hiring or growth position
4) Creating efficiencies in your job-search process to maximize your return on invested time and effort

What are the primary milestones in the process?

Before you begin your search, it is important to understand the fundamental steps and typical timelines of the job search process. Though it will vary slightly depending on the companies to which you are applying, the primary steps will occur as outlined below. Note that you will likely be doing many of these tasks simultaneously during the application period.

1. Research companies and industries of interest

2. Finalize resume
3. Find and develop contacts and network within the industry
4. Build a list of target companies
5. Search for online requisitions that fit your graduation timeline
6. Complete application and submit resume
7. Receive telephone contact and set up first-round phone interview
8. Interview one to two times by phone
9. Receive telephone call or email organizing a face-to-face interview
10. Interview one to two times face-to-face
11. Receive offer or indication that you were not selected
12. Complete background check

Companies have hiring timelines too:
Large corporations typically operate close to the following schedule to fill postgraduate jobs. It is important to note that major companies will often hire on this schedule, as well as an ad hoc basis. Smaller corporations tend to hire when they need to fill a position, rather than on a structured timetable. We have seen students hired from September to as late as the summer after their senior year.

Typical hiring timeline for a top job at a Fortune 100 company:

September: Previous summer interns interviewed for full-time positions; some have already been offered positions during the internship

September/October: External job requisitions posted on the company website
Early November: Requisitions closed
November: Candidates reviewed and first round of phone interviews conducted
Late November/December: Final in-person interviews are conducted
Late December/Early January: Applicants notified
Three weeks after offer is given: Accept/decline deadline, position is filled

(Please note that the above timeline **can shift one to five months**, depending on the company's recruitment cycle.)

This isn't the timeline for all companies:
The above timetable is an example of the schedule for a Fortune 100's most coveted positions. For most large companies, the process takes **at least one to two months** from the time of posting to the final offer. Smaller companies can, though they do not always, operate on a faster timeline to fill a position. It is key to monitor the companies' websites regularly for any job postings. Companies will sometimes re-post a position if they did not hire any of the interviewing candidates.

Tucker's timeline and path to his first position:
Seeking a rotational program to explore his interests within corporate finance and develop his leadership skills, Tucker applied to a Fortune 30 leadership development program at

a diversified manufacturer. Though the program was based in Southern California, the rotational structure afforded him the opportunity to travel and work at four different sites in six different business units during his first two years of employment. While Tucker was very fortunate to start his career in this position, it came after hundreds of applications. He estimates that he sent out over two hundred applications, from which he received five invitations to interview, and earned two final job offers. Roughly 1-2% of Tucker's applications were successful - something to keep in mind when building your list of target companies.

Representative timeline of Tucker's path to his first full-time position:

September: Target company identified and researched, requisition found online

October: Application submitted through the company's online application platform.

Early November: First-round phone interview conducted. This interview was held with three company employees (one manager, one human resources representative and one analyst). Tucker believed he did well explaining his school experiences and how they related to the position, but struggled in demonstrating his technical skills and his classes' applicability to the program. *Follow-up "thank you" email sent.*

Late November: In-person interview day. Tucker visited a Southern California company facility with roughly fifty candidates for the ten openings in the rotation program. The interview was hosted by a three-person panel and the questions were primarily situational. The interview lasted for roughly one hour with ten questions asked. During the interview, Tucker demonstrated his leadership aptitude but struggled, again, with some technical questions. *Follow-up "thank you" email sent.*

Early December: Tucker was notified of his selection. The selection notification was followed by a background check, a drug test and a reference check. Tucker had two weeks to accept or reject the offer. *Follow-up "thank you" email sent.*

When do they expect me to start?
Students should start the job search process **as soon as their senior year begins**. When filling entry-level positions, most companies understand the typical school year timeline and don't expect you to start in the role until after graduation. However, when companies need to fill spots on an ad hoc basis, they may try to accelerate their schedule. Sometimes, a position will list a start date during the school year, preventing you from being able to fill the position on that timeline – but ask about their flexibility on the date. This may put students in a tough position when explaining their availability constraints due to graduation. To prevent any confusion, during

your correspondence you must be clear on your potential start date.

Graduating in winter?

College seniors graduating in the winter are *sometimes* at a disadvantage as the larger organizations' recruiting process is structured to start seniors in the summer months. Therefore, while it is not impossible to apply as a winter graduate, there may be a delay until the summer to begin your employment. Again, be clear to all parties regarding your start date.

The process is time intensive!

The process of applying for positions is, at a minimum, as time-intensive as adding an additional class to your schedule. To properly approach the process you must prepare to spend between **two to four hours** daily on your search. It is important to properly structure your approach, set aside blocks of time each day for career search focus, and look for efficiencies in the process. Later in this section we will outline how to approach the process of submitting applications to maximize your time and minimize your errors.

Cast a wide net:

Though as we have stated, it is important to apply to positions that provide you with the best combination of your **interests and your strengths**, as a soon-to-be-graduate, it is just as important to cast your net wide by applying to many positions across several industries. Though your scope shouldn't be too wide, submitting a large number of applications will increase your chances to practice your interview skills.

Find a teammate for the process:
Embarking on such a time-intensive process is easier with an invested partner. Pairing with someone with equal job prospects will help you share ideas, practice interview questions, and help you stay dedicated to the career-search process. Before you begin the process, find a partner with the same career timeline, share your goals and keep each other accountable throughout the process.
Note about your friends and teammates: If you are introduced to a position through a professor or mentor, which you do not plan to take, you should never recommend another candidate to a hiring team. Suggesting another name will reflect poorly on both you and anyone you recommend!

The Importance of Staying Organized

Organizing your contacts:
In your career search, your contacts are how you measure your wealth. It is recommended that you keep an Excel spreadsheet of all the contacts that you've communicated or networked with in your job search. Organizing data this way will allow you to access points of contact much quicker and sort through your connections by industry. Additionally, organizing your contacts prevents you from completely forgetting a contact, or worse, confusing them with another contact.

If you organize and take notes on every contact with whom you engage, the file will enable you to remember specific details about these contacts, and develop a personal relationship with them. For example, Tucker was in contact with an account manager at a major defense contractor and while they were talking he told Tucker that he was a New England Patriots fan. Tucker took note of this and when Tucker contacted him a few weeks later he mentioned the Patriots. This shows the individual that you remember details and that you took a personal interest in them.

Aside from this isolated success, Tucker believes many opportunities were lost due to his failure to organize his contacts and timing effectively. Organization of his approach is the single area to which Tucker felt he should have devoted more time throughout the job search process. Keep this in mind when you are juggling many conversations with different contacts!

Note: Try to remember their children or spouse's name if your contact brings them up. People like to talk about their kids and it will mean a lot to them to see your remember their families.

Develop a contact log:
We recommend that you start your grid of contacts early. Below are the categories that should be highlighted in your log. We recommend that you build in Excel to help you keep your contacts organized.

- Company
- Name
- Level or title
- Number and email
- Communication history
- Personal details

Collect schoolwork samples throughout the process:

Quite a few organizations ask for work samples to be provided post-interview. Sometimes companies may send you a case analysis to complete on your own and be returned within a specific time period. While you're in the application process, make a conscious effort to find and collect your finest work samples.

Leading up to his senior year summer, Tucker had an interview with a commodities brokerage. After his interview the director asked Tucker to send his "most advanced Excel spreadsheet." At that time Tucker had not done any real work with Excel. After confessing that he couldn't immediately send a spreadsheet, Tucker was sent a writing prompt and told he had 48 hours to send it back. After the writing sample was submitted, the director called Tucker back and discussed the submission. Tucker was offered the internship but not before he had to defend his paper while the broker argued the other angle. Quantitative work or writing samples allow a recruiter to cut through your resume to truly see what kind of work you're capable of producing. Keep your best work pieces organized so you can easily call upon them.

Industry Analysis:

When prepping for an interview, being able to demonstrate a deep understanding of the industry is critical to your success. Time between resume batch submissions will allow you to visit the library, or find online databases that pertain to your industry of focus.

Take the time to understand the industry. It will serve you better in the long run and could grant you specific information to reference during an interview. Additionally, if you're going to work in a high-tech or manufacturing industry as any type of non-engineering employee, you will be most valuable to the organization when you can dive even an inch deep into the technical elements of the organization. Demonstrating an understanding of how the product works is a great advantage for your chances of advancing in an interview. In short, ***do not cut corners in your preparation***.

Keep up with the news:

As elementary as it sounds, be sure to read the financial press daily. The headlines will have different implications for different industries and it is important to be able to call upon these meanings when interviewing. As one example, Tucker had interviewed with a financial services company shortly after the AIG bailout. Without notice, and unrelated to other interview questions, they asked Tucker to walk them through what the bailout meant for their company. This question was in search of the following: does Tucker keep up on recent news; does he understand their business model; could he see how outside factors affect their business; could Tucker clearly demonstrate his thought process.

Students should also set **Google Alerts** bringing all news of a target company to their inbox. The alert will send you an email of the article in which the company is mentioned. Sometimes you will get one email a week, or several a day, but it is a quick way to scan all the public news for the industry you are studying.

Insider tip: One of our students was flown up for an interview with a brand name Pacific Northwest corporation and engaged in an all-day set of interviews for an incredible opportunity to serve on a brand management team. Somewhere in the dialogue the student mentioned that they were spending the current semester working on a company project for a Business capstone class. The company our student had researched was a major diversified financial holding company with a wide variety of investments across several distinct business fields. The senior manager jumped on this opportunity and started peppering the student with questions. The student did well in the answers, but then the senior manager said, "Well, why don't you go up to the board and show us the financials!" And, the student went up and did just that, working without notes. He got the job!

Insider tip: Another student, who had done his senior Business and Strategy capstone on a French technology company, was interviewing with the hiring manager for a top-rated commercial insurance carrier. The interviewer later told us that although he didn't personally know the first thing about the French company or anything about technology, he asked the student to explain the company and his capstone research because he figured if the student could do that clearly and concisely he would certainly be able to understand his company's products and explain them to possible customers! The student went on to get the position!

The moral of these two stories is that you should be ready to talk about the research you may have done in or outside of class, or experiences from the jobs and internships you have already held that pertain to companies or ways of doing business. If you have a good portfolio of experiences and know their content well, be sure to introduce that into the conversation at the appropriate moment. The moment would be with the hiring managers or others from the actual business unit, it would not likely be in early telephone interviews with human resources personnel.

Understanding You, Your Strengths and Your Goals

Strengths, Weaknesses, Interests and Perfect Job

In the process of finding the right career, a fundamental step is to identify your strengths, weaknesses and career interests. Tucker did not know what he wanted to do, but he knew his strengths, and figured that would be a good place to start. What did he enjoy? What were his strengths? Could there be a connection between his **strengths and early success** in a career? When starting his search, he wrote all his strengths as well as areas in which he struggles. Let's begin the process by listing out our Strengths, Weaknesses, Interests and Perfect Jobs (SWIP).

Tucker's SWIP:

Strengths:	Weaknesses:
• Communication skills • Financial analysis • Small group management • Ability to multi-task	• Computer/database design • Second languages • Technical/engineering understanding

Interests:	Perfect job: A position in corporate development for a renewable energy company.
• Sales • Financial markets • Renewable Energy • Early stage companies	What did this tell him? What are the paths? • Investment banking • Finance • Customer facing role • Strategy • Solar Energy/Renewable Energy

Why search for the "perfect job?"

Hopefully you are able to identify what your ideal job would be. If you're not sure where to start, begin with what you might envision as your perfect career. Tucker knew he was unlikely to find himself employed in his "perfect" career directly out of school, but he now had a list of different avenues that would incorporate his interests, both functionally and industry based.

Now, your turn to fill out the boxes below:

Strengths:	Weaknesses:
Interests:	Perfect job:

What do these four boxes tell you:

Understanding what you want in a career will help you find the "best" job:

After graduation, most will be advised to take the "best" job they are offered. The best job will typically provide you with the most opportunity to move forward in your career, either vertically or laterally within a company. But, what many fail to recognize is that you should try to narrow your search to jobs that will **combine your interests with your**

strengths. (Interests are the types of industries you want to work for). The best job is relative to each candidate; for some it may be the highest pay, for others the office environment, or the location, or a combination of all these. Whatever it may be, each candidate must be able to weigh what he or she finds most important in a career; the best place to start is in a growth industry where you have a deep interest.

What are some of your industries of interest? (E.g. advertising, health care, technology)

1. _____
2. _____
3. _____

The value of starting with a functional path, rather than an industry:

Companies value flexibility and a recent graduate's ability to understand many industries. If you are passionate about a functional path, (e.g. accounting, marketing, or sales), searching for careers based on a functional path will expand your list of target companies; every industry has an accounting or marketing path. If you are passionate about a skill set, but don't know what industry you are interested in, search for the position with the most leadership potential within the specific skill set. Gaining experience within a specific functional path will allow you to develop an understanding of your industries of interest while gaining invaluable on-the-job experience.

What are your targeted functional paths: (e.g. accounting, sales, operations, human resources, finance, etc.)

1. _____
2. _____
3. _____

What type of organizational style should I be seeking?

Now that we understand the fields of interest, fill out these "career style" questions to begin thinking about what organizational style might fit you best:

1. Do I like organizational structure or do I like to work under my own supervision?

   _____

2. Do I want a wide scope of responsibilities in the workplace or do I want to have a specific area of expertise?

   _____

3. Do I prefer to be a small part of a large group or a large part of a small group?

   _____

4. What do I really want to get out of my first two years of employment?

   _____

5. Do I like working on multiple projects at once or do I like singular focus?

   _____

6. What title do I want to hold?

   _____

Communicating your strengths:
Everyone has strengths that can be leveraged into a successful career. What are yours? Understanding your strengths is the first step in finding meaningful employment. As you begin the application process, we recommend looking for positions that align with your strengths rather than searching for jobs out of reach of your abilities or experience. Within these strengths, there are certain skillsets that you have the ability to highlight further.

As an example, let's create a sample student's strengths:

***Top-level strength*: "I am an effective communicator."** Effective communication is important for most careers, but simply stating this as a strength won't separate you from the competition. This strength must be demonstrated. Let's break that down and get more in depth:

Break down your overarching strength into specific skills that can be applied to a job requisition.

Level One: "I am an effective communicator"
Level Two: "I am able to maximize other's contributions and integrate their efforts into a common goal
Level Three: "I am effective in managing a small group by helping people work together"

By the time you drill down to the third level, you will identify a specific strength (level three above) and understand how to leverage that into success in an entry-level position. When setting up strengths, we recommend that you do this by **articulating your overarching quality** and then drilling down to identify aspects where you specialize so as to separate yourself in an interview. Do note that the interview panel will expect you to have a story ¬ or a specific example to prove the point.

Why is drilling down within your skillset important?

Drilling down within your skill-set is important because companies know that you could be an effective communicator but a poor salesperson, and explaining that you are an effective communicator won't win you a sales job. But by showing the recruiter that you are able to lead a team and that you are passionate about sales, you are able to directly explain your effectiveness in specific segments of sales roles in varying organizations. When you know your strengths, you can begin to understand which jobs are right for you and to identify which attributes of those strengths you want to leverage.

In the application, be sure to demonstrate key personal strengths and explain how you can use these skills to add value to their company.

Fill in the boxes below with your strength:

Overarching Strength: 1)	Specific Strengths: 1) 2)	Specific Applicable Skills: 1) 2) 3)

What is "Organizational Fit"?

Answering the questions above will allow you to begin to target and find jobs that will fit your preferences. Organizational fit is an environment that provides you the ability to work with like-minded people and feel comfortable with the culture. It is a social environment that facilitates the greatest personal development and team success. Work culture, hours, office environment and personal alignment with organizational goals are all components of finding organizational fit. Having worked in both large, structured companies as well as small, flexible organizations, we cannot stress enough the importance of finding your own best fit. Knowing what works for you will allow you to target organizations that best meet your needs and desires.

How a large organization can feel like a start-up:

Though many students seem to draw a mental line between big and small organizations, know that even if you work for a large Fortune 500 corporation, you will be working within a specific division and often on a small team or business unit. Although you may be a piece of a very large organization, the immediate environment can feel small, entrepreneurial and allow you to make decisions that drive the team in specific directions. Remember that large companies are made up of hundreds of small units that can provide new hires with the mentoring and personal guidance one might expect at a smaller organization.

Entrepreneurship & Internal-entrepreneurship:

Many students rightfully want to work in an entrepreneurial capacity and build their own business or process. Those seeking positions with even the largest companies will have the opportunity for internal-entrepreneurship within their division. Internal-entrepreneurship means developing and growing a product or system within a business. Companies seek self-starters who will change the way things are done. As a recent graduate, you will have the opportunity to work in an entrepreneurial capacity supporting your division.

What do you want to accomplish in two, five and ten years?

Considering that by the fall of senior year many still have little idea of where they will start their careers, we recommend establishing a two-, five- and ten-year plan of where you want to be. Setting professional goals must encompass the three primary pillars of one's career journey: **1) Professional, 2) Educational, and 3) Personal**. Writing down these goals is an important step to establish direction and structure your application process.

List your career goals!
It may be hard to identify descriptive two-, five- and ten-year goals, but there is a trick to start thinking about establishing realistic and stretch goals. Start by asking specific questions such as:

- How important is a dynamic work scope for you? _____
  (Challenging, flexible, non-repetitive)
- Where do you want to be living in 10 years? _____
- Do you want to manage people or do you see yourself more as a technical expert? _____
- What type of work/life balance do you want/expect to have? _____
- Do you prefer stability or risk?
  _____
- What type of role/influence do you want to have within the organization?
  _____
- Do you want to get a master's degree? If so, when? _____

List out your career goals for the next two years:
(Your goals can include a title you want to earn, or a skill you want to develop)
-
-
-
-
-

Additionally, list out your ten-year goals. These should be both career-based and personal milestones. Personal and professional goals are intertwined and should not be viewed in isolation.

List your ten-year goals below:

Personal:
Educational:
Professional:

What skills do you want to develop in the next two years?

There is a vital difference between taking an entry-level job to receive a paycheck and finding the right job that allows you to achieve your short and mid-term goals. After establishing your goals, you can begin to narrow down the type of jobs to which you should apply. Writing down your personal goals and work values that you deem important may seem hypothetical, abstract and difficult. However, aligning your applications with your goals will make you a better employee and more satisfied over time. You need to select an organization that can clearly offer you opportunities to achieve your goals. Decisions should be made based on the range of opportunities that the company will provide in the near future, and further down your career path, rather than on short-sighted metrics such as starting pay or prestige of the company. It should be noted that an organization *can* help you to accomplish your early career goals. We recommend that early in your career you **communicate your two-year goals** - If an organization does not work for you after two years it is always OK to transition to another opportunity.

If possible, it's great to plan many years in advance:

We have many examples of our highly successful graduates who have planned out their first ten to twenty years in the workplace. One graduate, who is today a very senior leader in a global fashion house, laid out all the functional and industry areas that he would need to acquire in order to become a fashion executive. To do this, he spent 18 years learning every aspect of finance for a global manufacturer and then went on to head the capital planning for a top retailer. Do note, of course, that once you go through your early career, your goals and ambitions will likely change. Though it is great to plan this many years in advance, it is also important to keep yourself flexible enough to take opportunities as they arise.

One opportunity leads to another!

Remember that one door truly opens another. We had a very talented senior whom we referred to a major investment house founded by an alumnus with whom we were well-acquainted. The student made an excellent impression on the founder, but there wasn't a position at the firm for an individual with the skill sets he possessed. So, what happened? The founder called a friend at

another investment bank and said, "I have
been talking with an exceptional candidate, but
we don't have a place at this time. I think you
should meet him." And that got the process
started for our student, with an even larger firm
that had more opportunities. Our student
interviewed well and was considered for an
opportunity, but he came in second. However,
one of the hiring managers told him, "Look, you
were the runner-up in a very tough competition.
We are going to seriously keep our eyes open
for other opportunities and bring you back in if
there is a match." Within three weeks the
senior was back interviewing again for another
position, and this time he got the job!

This story is provided to highlight that each
job can lead to another if you plan correctly.
While in your current position, you must keep
your eyes open to the skill sets you wish to
develop and the opportunities that are arising
around you. Be clear in what you want out of
your first job, what types of skill sets you want
to develop and what network you want to
create. With planning, your first career will
open the door to many opportunities two to
three years after graduation.

Selecting and Targeting Your Applications:

**How to identify the company's position in
the industry and understand why they are
hiring:**
When you find an open position, you must
first think, **why is this company hiring**? The
company may be hiring because they need to
fill an open position that will increase their

revenues, adjust to a new trend, or prepare for an increase in sales volume. Being able to understand a company's hiring cycles is key to building your story in an interview. Large companies (the Fortune 500) typically recruit a set number of high-potential candidates each year, and both large and small organizations add new grads on an ad hoc, as-needed basis.

Key questions to understand when you see a job posting:

- What are the general trends in the industry?
- What is happening in the economy as it relates to the industry and the company?
- What is happening with the technology or their key products?
- How do they compete within their market? How do they differentiate?
- Compared to their competitors, are they positioned well for growth in the next ten years?
- What is the company's edge?
- What do they do well/what do they need to improve upon?
- What are regulations doing to the industry and the company?
- Who are the competitors (current & potential); where are they most exposed to lose market share?
- How do people feel about working for this company?

Rotational Programs vs. Single Job Openings:

In the past decade, many large companies have embraced rotational programs in all fields (IT, Finance, Engineering, Human Resources) as an opportunity to give new hires the broadest knowledge about the company and allow them to discover their passions and interests within the organization. From the organization's perspective, it gives the company a metric of how you've performed in each different role and how you might fit into the different units' cultures.

These programs are typically one to three years long and structured to provide new hires the opportunity to rotate through three to eight different positions, divisions and functions. From a new hire perspective, with little understanding of what type of work you may want to do for the next ten years, rotational programs are a fantastic opportunity to explore various fields and gain a breadth of knowledge. When placing you in a final position after the rotation program, companies are looking for a match between your interests and how you performed and fit with each business unit. **Please Note:** Rotational programs typically require a 3.5 minimum GPA, and are highly competitive.

Conversely, being recruited to fill an individual position requires the new hire to jump in and work with a team specifically on one task for a year or longer.

Single job openings:

If you have applied for a specific job, as opposed to a rotational program, one of the most important questions you need to ask is, "Where do people who do very well at this position go next?" and "What are the career pathways for this position?" These are critical questions to find if success in this position will allow you to move forwards and upwards. We suggest asking these questions of the various interviewers you meet with, as their answers may provide different perspectives. You want to make sure that there is room for advancement, or that you will be able to gain knowledge that is highly transferable.

Know whom you'll be competing against:

A recent graduate we've coached was flown out to a set of interviews with a Fortune 100 company. The student found that all the other candidates were MBAs. How did he learn this? At a reception that was held the night before, he asked the other interviewees about their backgrounds. While this was intimidating, the student decided that there must have been a reason he, as the only non-MBA, was there. Although he didn't say anything directly about this, strategically he approached the interviews feeling confident that he could provide the employer with what they wanted, but not at the price tag of an MBA. He got the position, and turned out to receive a total compensation package that placed him in the top one percent of his graduating class.

When filling single-position openings on a team as opposed to in a rotational program, companies sometimes look to bring on the **brightest person at the lowest cost**. Knowing that you may be competing with MBAs for entry-level positions, it is your responsibility to demonstrate how, as a recent graduate, you will bring value to the organization and that you are flexible enough to be trained into a long-term company leader. Learn as much as you can about the types of candidates you will be competing against and strategize how to present yourself as the best value option.

Building a list of potential employers

After you have identified your interests, begin building a list of employers you may target for your applications. We recommend applying for *100 positions* in total. However, this total amount may vary based on your resume, target industries and existing connections. As stated earlier, Tucker applied to over 200 positions with about a 2% offer rate – your chances increase with the larger number of applications submitted!

Hoovers.com, likely available in your university library's database, is an effective site to identify a company and find all their competitors within the industry. Similar to Hoovers, **Mergentintellect.com** allows the user to aggregate companies based on industry, size and other metrics. Mergent has developed their own job board that consolidates positions from over 243 million tracked companies across the planet. **Bloomberg.com** also has an online database of all companies within specific industries and provides one of the most comprehensive lists on the web. Additionally, visiting a website like **Vault.com** allows you to search within a specific industry and sort by number of employees, or total revenues, for example.

The four steps for creating maximum efficiency:
To streamline the application and job-search process, we suggest breaking the application process into four periods. Our four-step process is outlined below:

1) **Step 1:** Find companies and specific requisitions or email submittal points of contact for potential applications
2) **Step 2:** Find specific points of contact at the target companies and let your advocates know your aggregated list
3) **Step 3:** Submit application
4) **Step 4:** Send follow-up emails

Step 1: Spend the first session creating an aggregate list of companies and specific links to their online requisitions or points of contact for email submittal. This is best done in a Word or Excel document.

Step 2: Search through these companies' home pages and find specific points of contact to whom you will address your application and your follow-up emails. Organizational structures are typically found in the "About" section on their website. This can most easily be done for smaller companies that may list their organizational structure, or at a minimum, their human resources department. For larger companies, it is not easy, if not impossible, to find specific points of contact. To do so, rely on your personal network or search regionally through local business journals and associations, as we discuss in the section on "location specific" career searches.

Step 3: On the third day submit a block of applications en masse. It is important to pay close attention to any updates to your resume or cover letter (if required by the company). Nothing looks worse than sending out a resume or cover letter addressed to the wrong person! After you submit, keep note of the companies that you've applied to by filling out a tracking spreadsheet. In this session, alert any personal contacts at these companies by letting them know that you've applied. We will go over building your database of contacts in the following chapters.

Step 4: Make sure you stay on the minds of your points of contact within the company. Three days after you submit your application, touch base. Explain that you have submitted an application and reiterate that you are extremely interested in the position.

This process isn't for everyone!
Be aware that this structured timeline will not work for everyone. Some students will be more likely to apply to positions in an ad hoc, unscheduled fashion, which is fine too. The goal of structuring your application submittal this way is to create efficiencies in the process

and increase the number of applications submitted, thus increasing your odds to move to the interview round.

Set a weekly schedule:
To stay on track in your job and internship search, set weekly goals and track your progress on a week-by-week schedule. Targets such as "five applications submitted" and "one informational interview held" will help you stay on track and manage yourself over the process. Have your career search partner keep you disciplined to this schedule.

A note about internal employee referrals:
Each company has their own policy on the process for employee referrals. Some companies (most small organizations fall into this category) have an open referral process where each employee can recommend an unlimited number of applicants. Others may have a one to two recommendation a year limit for each current employee. Often, companies will prohibit allowing vice presidents and other senior managers from recommending an applicant as they might unfairly influence a hiring decision. Though the job applicant has no control over the company's policy, it is something to understand when creating a relationship with an internal contact. Please note that most companies will prefer employee referrals as an opportunity to source top talent.

Cash awards within companies for recommending new hires:

Many companies across a wide variety of industries -- high technology, retail, consumer products, diversified conglomerates -- pay cash awards to their current employees for finding individuals who are ultimately hired. In some cases employees are paid a thousand dollars or more for referring the right person.

What does this mean for you? It could mean that you need to think carefully about any opportunity that a friend has referred you to, if that friend works in the same company, because they might not be objective when they share with you the glories of that particular work assignment. Be wary of the parameters and possible terms of the recommendation.

Use your university to help in the process

How to utilize on-campus career centers:

University career centers are a great place to start when building a list of online employers and mapping out all your contacts within an industry. The campus career center works closely with alumni relations and keeps tabs on graduates throughout many industries. Once you identify your field of interest, on-campus career centers will likely be able to provide you with a list of all university alumni working in that particular field, as well as help divide that list by geographic region. The career center can be an invaluable resource to assist in building your alumni network and can help you break into industries of interest through a university contact.

Consider taking a single class at a larger university:

If you attend a smaller university, there are ways to access the **larger alumni databases at surrounding universities**. It is recommended to enroll in at least one class at a nearby public university, if you feel their alumni base is worth leveraging. By enrolling in a class, you are usually entitled to use their career center and access their alumni connections. Of course, before enrolling in just any nearby university, consider their alumni network and how active alumni support is throughout the school.

Insider Tip: One recent graduate from a small liberal arts college took a single class at a major public university with at least 20,000 undergraduates and through that enrollment was able to gain interviews with a major worldwide computer chip manufacturer and a major medical software company. Obviously his resume consisted almost totally of his experiences gained through the small liberal arts college, but his enrollment at the larger university got his foot in the door through their alumni base.

Another student called other universities' career placement offices. She called two major California universities and simply asked for contact information for the recruiters of a specific Fortune 100 Pacific Northwest-based company. She got the contact information and sent each one his resume, with a note that read, "I feel I am very qualified to be considered for entry-level opportunities at your company and my resume explains why." The recruiter saw the value in the resume and today that student works for that Fortune 100 company.

Try Alumni Relations & key professors

If your career center isn't directly responsive or isn't able to assist you in your search, the next step is to contact the alumni relations department and ask for any contacts they may know in your target industries. When approaching the alumni relations staff, understand that this isn't a typical request, so be clear in your message and make it easy for them to help you. It is most important to do this face-to-face, to create the best opportunity for a helpful response.

The other avenue, with a higher chance of success, is to speak with your closest professors about your list of targeted companies. The professors can review your list and add any companies that might fall within your areas of interest. Additionally, they may suggest companies that have hired from your alma mater in the past, or where they have personal connections that may assist you in the application process.

What's a target school?

Each major corporation has target schools from which they actively recruit. They are sometimes required to fill a certain number of entry-level spots each year with students from these target universities. Target school status is often granted by close geographical location to these corporations, a prominent executive alumni base or a long history of recruiting with the university. Some companies only interview at some of their target schools, but have a larger set of schools designated within their recruiting software. This means that certain companies flag certain universities inside their system so a student can be automatically signaled for a review if they apply online even though they do not physically recruit at that university.

One major financial services corporation, for example, has two different recruiting processes which students are funneled into: Target and Non-Target applicants. All non-target applicants are competing for a limited few spots and may often need to go above and beyond the requirements of the target applicants. As an applicant, understand this in your process and explore which organizations may target your school in their hiring.

Is your university name not on the drop-down list?

Sometimes the requisition will have a drop-down list with a fixed number of universities listed. One student, encountering this drop-down with a major logistics company in the Fortune 100, was blocked from applying, as his university was not named. One of his professors told him to simply pick one of the universities on the list, any one, and submit his resume. He did so and he was called for an interview. Ten years later, he is now a rising executive in that company. If your school isn't on the list, apply anyway!

On-campus speakers and events:

Through on-campus clubs, the career services department and your major's department, there will be on-campus presentations, speakers and events. These occasions are a terrific way to expand your network and be introduced to industries and individuals in management or hiring positions. Attend these events, be engaged, and introduce yourself after the presentation to the speaker. If it seems appropriate, ask for a business card and thank them for their time. A few days later, follow up with that contact, thank them again, and share with them your interest in the industry and their specific company. The event sponsor (likely a department lead or a member of the development team) may have a personal connection with this contact and have insight if they are in a hiring position. It is recommended to touch base with the sponsor for the presentation as well, thank them and explain that you're interested in reaching out to the campus guest.

Career fairs:

Most universities will offer a spring career fair with local companies in attendance. Whether or not your university offers a fair, we recommend you visit all the available career fairs at neighboring universities. While this may be a low-yielding career-search tactic, visiting career fairs will help you practice talking with professional recruiters and presenting your resume. It is important to dress professionally as the booth recruiters can be the gatekeepers to more formal interviews. Bring twenty copies of your resume and a notepad. Most companies will just direct you to their online careers sites, but your resume should be brought in case of specific questions or unique opportunities.

Online resources

Though there are a plethora of online job postings, the trick is finding a search engine or a website that makes your time worthwhile. While we don't endorse the approach of relying heavily on search engines for requisition searches, when it comes to building a list of target companies, there are a number of worthwhile tools available to enhance your search:

- **LinkedIn.com - industry groups**
- **INC.com - fastest growing companies**
- **Fortune.com - best places to work**
- **Crunchbase.com - funding announcements**

LinkedIn:
LinkedIn is the most transparent of all career search websites. To post jobs, the company must have a legitimate and vetted user profile registered with LinkedIn. Typically, in these profiles, each company will have a comprehensive explanation of their business, their management and their industry.

LinkedIn Industry Groups:

Using LinkedIn allows you to select by industry and receive daily/weekly emails with industry job posts. These may be bothersome to receive daily but there is a way to filter for only job posts within your range of required experience and within a prescribed geographical location.

The value of LinkedIn Premium:

LinkedIn Premium allows the user to tap into the full potential of LinkedIn and the online groups. With Premium, the platform will allow you to directly contact users outside of your network. Additionally, it will allow the user to view those who have viewed your profile. LinkedIn Premium provides recruiters the platform to view all those on the Premium network, an advantage that is not realized on a traditional LinkedIn account. The pricing is $30 per month, and surely worth the investment. Your university may have a discount available to students.

How to utilize LinkedIn to contact someone outside your network

LinkedIn is a fantastic tool for those initiating a job search. What LinkedIn does is expand the base of people to those you *do not already know*. Through the "people you may know" tool, LinkedIn allows a job seeker to search for second-connection contacts through their immediate network.

LinkedIn Groups are for the most part, open to anyone. Joining a group instantly gives you a network of professionals working within the industry you hope to enter. When entering a LinkedIn group, find the specific targets of your search and reach out to them with a personal email. This tactic may be limited to certain groups but it is certainly available in all industries if you subscribe to LinkedIn Premium.

How to introduce yourself cold over email:
Emailing the newly developed contact is a delicate situation, (the internet's form of cold calling). These two techniques will typically yield zero response:

1. Only introducing yourself
2. Asking for a job

Rather, you must go to them with a request, something that **demonstrates your interest and does not require much effort on their end**. You must show sincere interest in their job and their opinion of what it would take to enter the industry. Remember, when you ask for advice, people become invested in you.

Be sure to introduce yourself professionally, taking care not to sound like a desperate student seeking a job and looking to use them to get there. A sample LinkedIn contact email to use in contacting the LinkedIn group member:

Hello Mr. Smith,

I hope this message finds you well. I am Janet Job Seeker, a senior at the University of _____ in (location). I am in my final year of study focusing on _____ and _____. (*This is where you can tailor it specifically to their job title.*) I am writing you today to express my interest in your work with _____. It is my goal to enter the _____ industry and I am looking for different ways to research and network within the industry. I understand you must be very busy but I wanted to ask you if I would be able to set up a quick informational call and ask you a few questions about your job, the requirements of the industry and any advice for a student looking to enter the industry. I appreciate your time.

My Very Best,
Janet Jobseeker

You will be surprised how much people like to talk about their accomplishments, particularly when communicating with someone who demonstrates interest in their current position. If approached correctly, a first conversation can start a domino effect and down the road you may be speaking with someone in a hiring position. Remember, **don't directly ask these new contacts for a job!**

Insider Tip: Early in Tucker's career search he joined several Solar Energy industry groups to learn more about the market and specifically about the type of professionals that have made careers in this field. Upon joining an industry group, you are granted access to the profiles of all group members. After his due diligence into a few of the companies, Tucker reached out to individuals working in the sales departments of the major solar panel manufacturers. He explained that he was an eager student looking to learn more about their industry, and even though he was emailing them cold, Tucker had several responses offering to discuss the market over email or in a short phone call.

He prepared for these conversations by studying both their profiles and their companies to have plenty of background to prepare for their dialogue. To his surprise, these complete strangers not only made themselves available to discuss the industry and their company, but even offered to put in a good word with the hiring manager after he submitted his resume.

Though online career tools can seem impersonal and public, your ability to join industry groups will give you a smaller and more intimate network to utilize in your search. It is important to note that though Tucker's story referenced the solar energy industry, this tactic can be used for making connections in all industries.

Other tools for finding which companies are hiring:

INC.com

There is an obvious benefit to applying to the companies listed on the "fastest growing companies." The **INC 500** fastest growing companies list provides you with a 360-degree view of what these companies do and what type of positions they'll need to fill. INC 500's company pages give a background description, areas of growth and growth projections. This list is invaluable for the college job seeker. This is the most comprehensive list on the web for companies looking to expand and likely to hire. The list also allows you to search by industry, a huge advantage to job seekers looking to enter a specific field. This year, INC 500 created their own job board. This is a job board for postings for the 500 fastest-growing companies in America. Of all the companies in the United States, this list provides you with the ones that are **most likely to hire.**

Crunchbase.com

If you want to work for a start-up, visit crunchbase.com and look for companies that are receiving funding from venture capital or private investors. Crunchbase's main page lists companies that have received investments from venture capital, private equity or institutional investors in the past month. When companies are expanding financially, they are also expanding their employee headcount. You can even contact these companies stating that you have been following their development and you feel that you can help them going forward.

Keep your eyes open: If you hear about a company in the news landing a big funding round, look online for an increase in job postings. This goes beyond start-ups. **Note**: If you pay attention to what is going on in the macro economy, you will see trends in specific industries and be able to predict which industries, and even companies, are positioned for growth.

Industry Job Boards

If you are targeting a specific industry, the industry job boards are a great way to search for a variety of jobs within that sector. Our students have used job boards such as **malakye.com** to find positions in targeted niche industries. A simple Google search can lead to job board sites for most industries.

Warning: be wary of contingency recruiters

Contingency recruiters will occasionally contact an applicant. Traditionally, the types of roles they are soliciting for are high-turnover sales roles. Be wary of these recruiters, as they will often place you for a commission in a low-growth company. Similarly, they may refer your resume to a company where you are already interviewing or plan to be interviewed. If they submit your resume it could potentially add to the confusion with the company and tarnish your image with their recruiting office.

Not-for-profits, NGOs, and Federal, State and Local Governments

A subgroup of our readers will have an interest in finding employment with a not-for-profit organization or a government organization. Many of the examples we offer are applicable, in terms of building a path towards employment through activities on campus and internships, although the types of activities you may choose to pursue will differ.

112

Many corporations will be equally as interested in you as a candidate if you have held an internship with a government organization during your junior summer, as all of the opportunities described below are highly competitive. For example, we have had students work as interns for the U.S. Department of Commerce, the U.S. Department of Justice and the U.S. State Department regionally and overseas. All of those students ultimately went on to find great jobs, upon graduation, with major U.S. Corporations.

Not-for-profits and NGO's:
In a perfect world, if you are seeking to be involved with not-for-profits or NGOs that serve the common good of the world, or specific communities, you will find opportunities as early as possible to volunteer your services. This will establish a track record of service, about which you can speak with interviewers. The record must demonstrate that you give your time and energy to assist others. Almost every university in the United States has service programs in which you can get directly involved, that provide support to elementary education, hospitals and high schools. These are not situations solely for students wanting to be teachers or nurses, and these organizations are typically very happy to receive support from all types of students and thus encourage the involvement of students from all majors. As you advance in your academic training, you may find specific examples of fieldwork for which you are qualified that will offer you the

opportunity to work as an assistant outside your institution, either within the United States or in an overseas setting.

We have had students work in a variety of not-for-profits and NGO's ranging from the traditional Teach for America and the U.S. Peace Corps, to much more specialized organizations focusing on environmental, health care and educational issues in the developing world. Do note that in some cases, some foreign language ability may be required, though most of these organizations understand that as an undergraduate, unless you are a heritage speaker, you may not yet be proficient.

The best way to get started is to talk with your professors and see if they know of any faculty who might be working to help others either at home or abroad. Some of our students have worked on GIS and Environmental Studies issues in Mexico, while other have worked on Communicative Disorders in Guatemala, while still others have volunteered for a summer of service in a wide variety of nations, including Cambodia, Chile, Honduras, South Africa, Ghana, Paraguay, Nepal, Nicaragua, Panama, Peru, Thailand and Vietnam, to name only a few. The opportunities are certainly out there. We strongly recommend that you speak to your professors and administrators involved in overseas studies, as they will be able to point you towards programs that will have proven reliable for your institution.

Governments at all levels:

As for employment with governments, go to your state government's website and check out the fields of service that interest you. The most comprehensive websites, like CA.gov (California's state site), offer you a chance to browse and check out the salaries of various types of jobs before you apply. You can also register with many states and place your profile online so that they will be able to access your file and notify you when opportunities come available. Many state and county websites operate in a similar fashion.

We would also recommend, if you think you have an interest in working for the government, that early during your junior year of college, after identifying appropriate opportunities, you visit your state representative's office. By state representatives we mean elected assembly or senators who serve at the State Capitol, not Washington DC. Most of the internships they have will be ones you will apply for that year, for the summer before your senior year.

Beyond the federal government offices, almost all states will have two state representatives, one for the lower and one for the upper house of state government, who are responsible for your hometown. These are the offices you want to visit. We also suggest you visit your hometown mayor's office. The idea is to find someone on the staff to speak with and to share with them who you are and the fact that you are hoping to find an internship with a government organization. They may be able to help you, but you should come prepared to show them what you have already done in terms of researching and identifying opportunities.

Jobs at the national level:
If you are looking for internships or jobs in Washington D.C., start by selecting a government bureau, agency or department that is of interest to you. For example, the U.S. Department of Commerce, which is responsible for promoting industry and commerce within the United States, as well as overseas trade, has a very typical website, www.commerce.gov, where you can find internships and recent-graduate jobs.

If you are interested in international internship assignments, you might start with the U.S. Department of Commerce, or the U.S. Department of State, at www.state.gov/initiative, or Foreign Service internships, which offer 8- to 10-week full-time placements. Another option might be the Environmental Protection Agency, at www.epa.gov/internship.

Now, the government can offer you many opportunities, but as we noted earlier, these are highly competitive. If you are looking at any particular internship or career-path employment, we also recommend that you check out what Glassdoor.com has to say about that organization. If it turns out you are interested in an opportunity in Washington D.C. or with a national organization in your local area, you still have to start with the national agency or departments' website.

Location-specific career searches

Local business journals:

Each major city has a local business journal that highlights the major news within the local industry. If you are looking for employment in a particular city, search for its local industry journals to keep abreast on the development or expansion of business within that region. These journals will often disclose if there is going to be a plant expansion, or a large-scale hiring effort in a local business unit. If you see this type of news, check to see what type of entry-level positions are looking to be filled and if they've posted the positions online. Company-opening announcements in specific regions will often list the key executives managing the expansion. Applicants with a strong desire to work in a particular region can contact these executives directly, by email or letter, and explain their interest in their organization. In your note to these executives, explain both why you want to work for this company and why you want to live in the region. They may be honored by your pride in the community and thus be more open to considering your application. They will all recognize the initiative you have shown in contacting them directly.

Local Chambers of Commerce and Rotary Clubs:

In addition to local business journals, if you're interested in staying within a specific geographical region, it is recommended that you check with the local Chambers of

Commerce for any updates on the local industry. The Chambers of Commerce are staffed with executives from local businesses and are a great place to expand your network. The Chambers of Commerce and local Rotary Clubs will have volunteer opportunities that will allow you to meet and greet local business leaders. This approach is highly recommended if you choose to apply to one specific region and can easily access these events in person.

Young Professionals Organizations:
Similar to attending events at the Chambers of Commerce, if you are looking to apply within one specific region we recommend you join the young professionals networks within that city. Though these groups might not contain local executives, it will be a way to hear about position openings and network with peers.
Meetup.com is an effective online channel to find young professional organizations. Meetup will often post an event within each city and allow you to find networking opportunities with local peers in a social setting.

Summary:
Your diligence in the preparation period lays the groundwork for your success in subsequent sections. The first steps we just walked through take time, planning and your undivided attention. Allowing yourself time to figure out what you truly want in a position will give you a head start in the application and interview processes, and set the platform for a successful career. Now that you understand your talents, have identified near- and long-

term goals, and built a list of potential
employers, let's move on to Section III, The
Application.

Section III – The Application

In this section we cover, in detail, the process of submitting the application. There are a number of important steps prior to hitting the send button that we will cover in this chapter such as:

1. Carefully reading the job description
2. Organizing the required material for submittal
3. Beating the resume filters

The Job Description

Reading a job description thoroughly and correctly is critical. Understanding the job description in detail will **allow you to tailor your experiences and make yourself more competitive in the application and interview**. Be sure to carefully analyze their description and strategize how you will tie your experiences in to their requirements. Don't let *any piece* of the job description go unnoticed.

First step is to understand the nature of the company for which you are targeting for an application:

- Are they large or small?
- Do they have a broad portfolio or a specific product?
- Are they in a period of growth or stagnation?

- How is the economy changing the space in which they operate?
- What type of attributes would you seek in employees if you managed this company?

Thoroughly read the description:
Application submittal is not a cookie-cutter process. Understanding this and being able to tailor your four years of college experiences to each individual application will make you a very attractive candidate. Realize that everyone has some past experiences that they can draw on to answer most direct questions in a job interview.

Read a little closer as to what they are specifically outlining in the requisition. Often, there will be keywords that deserve your attention. For example: ***flexible, team player, analytical***. Understanding and addressing these main points of interest to the company will set you above the rest of the competition. Be sure to understand the requests of the position when you are applying. Have those three to five traits mentioned on the requisition memorized and be able to demonstrate them through your submitted application and your interview examples. It is important to show that you possess their desired traits and that you took the time to understand what they seek in an applicant.

The different sections of the job description:

Typically, there are two different types of job descriptions you will find online. Smaller companies most likely will post the title of the job and a few lines about requirements (College graduate, experience with small team leadership, etc.). Smaller companies will also likely request that applicants send a resume and any required attachments to their email address, rather than upload to a online job page.

Larger companies typically have a much more formal and thorough job description page. As an example, the organization will typically have a job posting broken out into three sections:

1. **Position description**
   a. Job tasks
   b. Day-to-day responsibilities
   c. Organization you will support (Divisional Structure)
2. **Application Requirements**
   a. Educational
   b. Skillset requirements (fast learner, strong communication, etc.)
   c. Professional experiences or yearly experience minimums
   d. Location/Personal (Visas, security clearances, etc.)
3. **Requisition Description**
   a. Due date & method of submitting an application

Sometimes there won't be much information:

Sometimes, smaller companies will only post the basics of the position description. This will require you to do due diligence to understand what the position will entail. With smaller companies, if you are particularly interested, you might call them for more information regarding the requisition. Additionally, visit glassdoor.com and other user-generated sites to understand the company and any specifics on the position.

Addressing the requirements that you do not meet:

The dreaded line: **2 years experience required**. Though overcoming this requirement is a daunting task, it is not a definite dismissal of your application if you lack two consecutive years. When applying to a requisition that asks for more experience than you possess, **recognize that requirement and realize your resume must exceed their requirements in other categories**. Keep in mind that you should not waste time on submitting applications to positions where you *absolutely* don't meet their requirements. While some entry-level positions require two years of actual workplace experience, often students will have enough time spent through summer employment or internships to justify meeting the two-year experience mark.

Direct experience requirements are used to eliminate applicants that have no relatable experiences to bring to the position. The trick is to recognize that you don't technically meet the requirements, and to show that the other skills you are bringing to the company make you an equally attractive candidate. The interviewing team is looking at your resume and candidacy from a holistic perspective and will view your profile as an entire package.

Use those buzzwords!

In the past decade there has been an integration of online resume filters to cut down on time for first-round application screening. These resume filters are designed to prevent you from advancing to the next stage where an actual person will view your resume. The filters are designed to be **difficult to navigate and rigid**.

The computer filter will search for specific words listed on your resume. While reading the job description, look for key words in the desired applicants profile. **Matching your wording to specific words listed on the requisition** will often allow you to pass through the filter and onto the next step of having a representative review your resume.

On your application, make everything extremely clear. Have a clear GPA, graduation date, major and concentration of study. To get through these filters, you need to break down your application to its basics and **focus on clarity.** If you leave out dates of past experiences, or your GPA, your application will likely fail to make it through the filters. Though we recommend having one standard resume, it is important to leave it flexible enough to include key words from the job description to be flagged in the filter.

Submitting your resume:

There are two types of platforms that companies use to scan and review resumes. Either they have the traditional **upload document button** or, as seen for most large organizations, their sites may have a **text box** for you to paste your resume. If you are uploading, it is important to **upload resumes only in PDF format,** not Microsoft Word. PDF versions are seen as much more final and cannot be altered. Additionally, PDF versions prevent the reader from seeing any grammatical (red or green) error lines as they appear in Microsoft Word documents.

If you are submitting your resume by pasting it into a text box (as many larger companies provide), be sure to have and use an alternate copy of your traditional resume. This version of your resume will have everything **left aligned** and no unnecessary spaces. Pasting in your standard formatted resume, with some parts centered, some indented, and some right-spaced will alter the alignment when inserted and look unprofessional. Keep two versions of your resume, one primary (for upload) and one "left aligned" for you to copy and paste.

The non-template application:

While many large companies will have dedicated webpages for the application, many small companies will have you email your resume to the human resources representative. Though it might seem that this is less effort-intensive than an online form, significant time must be dedicated to wording the introductory email correctly.

Keep your introductory email short and direct the reader to your resume attached. Though the introductory paragraph won't win you an interview on its own, it is important to demonstrate professionalism throughout your entire application.

Example introduction for the text body of your email:

Dear _____ (find the (first) name of the person this should be addressed to):

I am writing to express my interest in the position of _____ with _____. I am Janet Jobseeker, a _____ studying _____ at the University of _____ in _____. Outside of my studies, I have held competitive internships with _____ and _____ and leadership roles with on-campus clubs. Please find my CV attached. I am very excited for this opportunity.

Thank you for your time,
Janet Jobseeker

If you don't have previous internships, apply anyway:

Remember, it's fine if you don't have previous internships! In that line of the email you can list any relatable summer positions or clubs in which you've participated.

Cover Letter: To include or not to include?

When submitting your application, be aware if they request a cover letter or only a resume. The majority of companies, particularly smaller organizations, will provide an email address and state, "please send your resume to the following email." If a cover letter is requested, submit your one-page letter as an attachment. If no cover letter is requested, we recommend you **don't attach an unsolicited cover letter**. The company will likely not read the cover letter and if anything, the additional words may hurt your application. Regardless of what is attached, you must write a professional message in the body of the email.

If you do choose to include a cover letter, make sure it gives information that is slightly different from your resume and is specifically aligned with the description. The letter will allow you to provide a more personal touch to the application and tell your story by including lines such as, "I'm very excited to return to (insert city)." Remember, if your resume is not strong, they **will likely not read your cover letter**. Likewise, a strong cover letter will rarely make up for a weak resume!

Summary:

Section III outlined the application process in your career search. Often students fail to truly understand what the requisition is asking for, and how to tailor their application approach. Identifying the requirements and desired skills from the requisition will separate you from the majority of other applicants who fail to specifically and comprehensively address the requisition in their application and interview. Read and re-read the requisition for a practical understanding of what the organization is seeking in an applicant!

Section IV - The Interview

Section IV details the interview structures of both large and small organizations. This section also covers, in depth, interview preparation techniques and your required "must dos" that will lead to a successful interview session.

The interview goes beyond the questions:
Interviews are important because they can teach the interviewer more about you than the highlighted words on the resume. When sitting in the chair in front of the interviewer(s), remember that they already have your resume in front of them. While your experiences could impress them, **the interview is designed to understand how you think, work through problems and react to different situations**. You will be wasting your time in an interview if you just rehash your resume! Tell the interviewer something that they can't see on paper. At the same time, it is important to tie the interview questions back to your experiences as outlined on the resume, so don't entirely depart from the application that got you to the interview.

Though you wouldn't think of it, they are actually screening for much more than the story addressed in your situational example. For instance, does this person follow directions?

When asked the following: *"Tell me about a time when you took responsibility for a group project"* the interviewer will be evaluating if you:

1. Can **follow directions** by answering the question in the requested format (situational question format outlined later in this section).
2. Know what your story says. If you acknowledge that you made a mistake, you show that you have the ability to recognize and address your errors and move forward.

Remember, during an interview, you are being evaluated on the **entire experience** you provide the interviewers. Your interview score is not limited to your story but also the traits you explain through the story, your demonstrated ability, your persona and body language, and your ability to respond directly to the questions asked.

Through answering a situational question, the interviewers are able to evaluate you in a number of categories:

1) Your story
2) Your ability to follow instructions and answer in the requested structure
3) Your personality traits presented through your stories
4) Your ability to express yourself clearly and concisely

Understanding the organization, your role, and your hosts

Understanding and adapting to the "Organizational Feel":

When going into an interview, it is of primary importance to understand and tailor your stories to the organizational structure and feel of the job for which you are applying. You need to slightly alter your responses for the different interviews. The in-person interview is a way for you to show "who you are" outside of your resume and it is very important to demonstrate how you will fit into the organizational culture. Knowing that you will be judged by how well the interviewer thinks you may fit within an organization, it is important to **mirror their tone** during an interview. If they are serious and approach the interview in a structured manner, it is necessary that you respond with answers in a similar fashion. On the other hand, if they are more conversational, try to conduct the interview in a less formal nature, while still driving home your abilities and your aptitude for the position. Understanding the company's organizational culture is just another way of demonstrating your emotional intelligence and your preparation for the interview. **Note**: Never get too relaxed. Even if the interview seems very conversational, treat the process with respect and keep your answers professional.

The importance of personality fit:

Interviews are often designed to discover your personality more than to audit your experience. Your resume will show you what you have done for the past four years, but the real question the interviewers want to figure out is if they would ***want to spend their entire day with you***. The interviewers will expect that if your resume has gotten you this far, your experience and technical background must be sufficient. If you are going to sit with someone for ten hours a day, you want to be able to respect them, enjoy their company and find some similarities.

Keep the pace cautiously casual:
One of the biggest problems with interviews is how nervous you may become. When you are nervous you might tend to speak too quickly or become robotic, preventing your true personality to shine through. Though it is an intense, high-stress environment, be able to show the interview panel who you really are: Be yourself, and ***be real***. You can also show your personality by keeping the interview friendly and casual (but not too casual!). There will be a number of points for "breaks" during the interview which are the perfect times for casual, but serious, small talk. You don't want to go silent as soon as the questions are over, but rather, have a conversation while waiting for the interview to begin or during breaks. Have a dialogue about the office, the surrounding area, and your time in the city; these are all safe topics. You are a guest in their office and city – be complimentary! It is important to remember that these people hosting the interview are, similar to you, likely **not enjoying the rigid structure** and hoping to get to know you on a personal level.

Understanding who will be hosting the interview:
Different from the in-person interview, the first-round interview will likely be conducted over the phone and handled solely by a human

resources manager. Be aware of this dynamic as you interview and provide answers. Though they may not know the exact position as well as the division manager, the human resources managers are looking for you to fit within the "box" of the requisition as well as be a cultural company fit. They will likely be interested in understanding your knowledge of the industry and why you are interested in working with their specific company. Some form of the question, "**Why do you want to work in this industry?**" will most certainly come up when interviewing with a human resources manager.

Interviews can be hosted by a variety of people within the organization. For the formal, in-person interview, it will likely be a panel with a range of representatives. Though companies of different sizes will vary in their approach, most typically the interview panel includes a manager from the division for which you are applying and a human resources representative. Occasionally, there will be an analyst or a younger employee in the room as well.

Though the interviewers are primarily asking the same questions, they will be evaluating different aspects of your answer. What will they look for?

- The hiring manager will likely be looking to see if you are someone who can be coached, grow within an organization and add value early to their team. Considering that they will likely be working with you on a day-to-day basis they will keenly be evaluating your personality.

- The human resources representative will evaluate how you answer the questions, how you may fit within their profile of what they are looking for and how your experience stacks up against other candidates.
- The younger or lower-level employee will be eager to know your personality, how you may fit with their current team, and how you might be to work with on a day-to-day basis. The lower-level teammate will likely be less focused on your past experiences and more focused on your mentality and personality type.

It is important to be cautious of the dynamics presented by a range of interviewers and understand how you might address each individual need with your answers.

Some details to understand regarding the day of the interview:
Face-to-face interviews will range from one to three hours to a full day. If you are flown out for an interview, you can expect the process to last several hours. It is always fine to ask the company representative arranging the interviews for details or a schedule. You may ask the following:

- Who will be interviewing and what are their titles?
- How long will the interviews last?

- How long will the process take altogether?
- Will there be one-on-one interviews, or will I be interviewed by a panel?
- Will I be interviewed by any of the people with whom I will be working?

The idea is to try and learn as much about the process as possible. Sometimes the person arranging the interview will not know all the answers, so always be careful not to push too hard.

Do your homework:
One of the ways Tucker impressed during his interview with an information services company (and what he believed to be a factor in landing a job offer) was the interviewer's ability to *see that Tucker **had prepared***. He was able to research beforehand the woman that would be interviewing him (He found her on LinkedIn). Tucker learned that she was a math major at a major Northeast University. In his interview question section, Tucker said, "If you were graduating University with your math degree today, what would you look for in a first position?" By putting in his due diligence and demonstrating his knowledge in an interview, Tucker was able to show the panel that he had worked hard to research and prepare. Don't overly research to a point of being obnoxious, but be sure to make it clear that you **have done your homework**.

Situational awareness:

Situational awareness is paramount during the start of an interview. It is important to judge and respond to what kind of person you think they are, and what type of examples or tone they'll desire. **Delivery** and timing are also key. If you are walking around the building and talking, don't deliver a scripted interview answer. Try to speak in a straightforward, but conversational manner. Demonstrate your emotional intelligence and adapt to your surroundings by mirroring the host's tone. The first portion of the interview will give you the idea of who the interviewer is, what type of organization you are in and how to proceed with your answers.

What should you bring to the interview?
- Classic and conservative binder or "padfolio" (avoid bringing laptops, iPads or other electronics unless explicitly requested)
- Six copies of your resume (Bring more than you expect you will need)
  - Bring resumes printed on **thick resume paper** (this can be found at any office goods store, or at FedEx/Kinkos
- Two to three pens
- Any exceptional college work (reports, capstones, honors thesis) – likely not requested, but good to have available.
- Transcripts (they may come in handy if requested) – the companies will notify you if these are requested

- A Tide (bleach) Pen in case of any spills prior to the interview!

The interview process takes time:
As a general rule, the better the job opportunity, the more complex the process and the greater number of interviews that you may encounter. For one of our students the interview process took over four months and consisted of a personality test, multiple tape-recorded interviews with the hiring manager and interviews in three different states, to which he was flown by the company. Our student had opportunities to speak with current employees in the position for which he was applying, two ride-a-longs/job-shadowing days, ten reference checks, a background check, drug test and even an interview with the candidate's fiancée and parents.

During the process, the student came back for advice multiple times not only for interviews, but also how to evaluate the opportunity against others available. We advised the candidate to find others in the same profession, but from other companies, who would be willing to talk about their experience in the profession, their path, and what they thought of the opportunity the candidate was pursuing. Some of the contacts were suggested to the candidate and others he found on his own. He was amazed at how willing these seasoned professionals were to meet and share their experiences! Ultimately, these due-diligence interviews convinced the candidate that he had found a truly unique and special opportunity.

He remains with his original employer to this day.

Don't share your interview with the world!
Though it should go without saying, avoid posting on any social media sites that you are interviewing with various companies. Recruiters will be monitoring your online presence from the moment you are extended the interview and peers may not have had the same opportunities provided by shared mentors.

The Formal Interview: Structure and preparation

Some companies use the behavioral-based method and some use much more abstract interview techniques. Visit **glassdoor.com** to assess what type of interview to prepare for and what type of questions may be asked. For most public companies, and many privates too, glassdoor offers insights into their interview structure which will help your preparation.

The standard breakdown of a Fortune 100 final interview:
- 15% introductions and specific questions about your resume
- 60% behavioral-based questions (potentially technical questions, depending on the industry)
- 15% questions directed towards the interviewer
- 10% conclusions or "next steps"

Know your resume:

Being able to understand the detail of your resume and detail of the job description will help you seamlessly intertwine your skill-set and experiences with the needs of the job. Be prepared to have detailed answers, experiences and examples of what you've learned related to each line item on your resume. Don't expect the interviewers to always focus on your most recent, or most important position! Tucker had an interview experience where over half of the interview as spent on a single bullet. Be flexible in your ability to use all **the experiences** on your resume in the interview.

Know the position description:

In some cases, the recruiters will be interviewing all day for a number of requisitions in their company. This will be particularly true for large corporations and especially for rotation programs. Due to the sheer volume that they'll have to review, the only thing they may know about the position is the posted requisition description. As an interviewee, you should try and **connect to this description** as much and as often as possible. If the description says it requires great communication, you should demonstrate that communication is one of your greatest strengths. It's fine to reference the requisition and explain that those qualitative characteristics are what initially drove you to be attracted to the position. Again, as we've mentioned before: **Always connect to the**

requisition and the position description, and link it to specifics on your resume.

Example: Tying the question back to the requisition description:

Company XYZ requisition reads: *Successful candidates will possess great: communication, teamwork and analytical skills.*

Question: *Tell me about a time when you improved a process at work?*

Example Answer: In my first internship I was given the task of ordering the parts for a signboard from a number of different suppliers. I noticed and calculated that the signboard part prices were outdated, and that we would be able to get better prices if we worked with just one provider of these signboard parts. I went to my teammates and asked about the current processes and discussed the last update of these processes. Through communicating with my teammates I was able to understand which partners were unreliable versus who had a great track record. After communicating and evaluating the situation I was able to determine that it would be more cost efficient to go with the single supplier, in bulk, rather than go to many individual parties. Through communicating with my teammates and analyzing the existing data, I was able to save the company 25% through this process improvement.

Through this answer the **following were demonstrated**:
- Analytical Skills
- Communication
- Teamwork
- Execution
- Ability to quantify an improvement

Practice answering the question below for a job description requesting the above skillsets:

Question: Tell me about a time when you have improved a process at your work or in the classroom?

Answer:

Confidence is key!

The single biggest impediment to a successful interview is the student's lack of confidence in the interview room. It is challenging to explain a step-by-step formula for building your confidence in an interview, so we will provide some basics that we believe can help build your confidence.

- ✓ Practice, practice, practice – those who feel they are most prepared often do the best when in the interviewer's chair.
- ✓ Take a business speech class. This will help you build presentation techniques.

- ✓ Understand that the company doesn't expect you to be perfect, and the interviewers aren't perfect.
- ✓ Know you are interviewing them just as much as they are interviewing you. It is important to find a mutual fit between yourself and the company.
- ✓ Remember: they're people, too! The interviewing team doesn't want to make you feel uncomfortable, they simply just want to get to know you and see if you will be a good fit with their company.
- ✓ You've made it this far. You've already been selected from a number of applicants so you must be doing something right!

Interviewing is all about practice. The more experience you have, the easier it will become. It is not a natural skill for anyone, so it is important to just relax, smile, and be yourself.

Interviewing as practice:
 Interviewing is a skill that needs to be practiced. If you are offered an interview, either through your own applications, or on-campus through your department, **accept the offer**. Even if you are not interested in the position, be sure to interview as many times as possible. The more you experience sitting in the interview chair, the more you will be able to hone your skills and prepare for the interview for the position that you really want!

Interview with someone who scares you!

It is very important that you start as early as possible to make contact and talk with people who scare or intimidate you. The more you do this the less intimidating you will find your interviewers. But where do you find intimidating people to speak with? Book a meeting with the president of your university, or the Dean of Students, the local Chief of Police, or the coach of your varsity football or other sports team. Develop some key questions that you want to ask the intimidating person. Also, be prepared to talk about yourself, who you are and why you are there to see them.

Many universities offer a speech or business speech lower-division course that will help you gain confidence through practice and organizing your thoughts. At the end of the day, the more that you can push yourself into any situation that requires your speaking to strangers, the better you will do when you have to interview for that internship or job opportunity. In fact, when you start looking for internships or jobs, even if it is a situation that you don't think you would want, try to get the interview, as it will be great practice for you and will help you gain confidence so that when the right opportunity presents itself you are ready.

Control your nerves!

One of our students, who had an impressive resume and seemed very well qualified for the position for which he was interviewing, was extremely nervous during his interview. The hiring manager was concerned that the student, if hired, might not be able to handle some of the leadership aspects of the position. The hiring manager shared these concerns with the employee who had recommended the student. "He has a great resume and he has had an excellent internship with a major corporation and his references are very strong. But he just seemed so nervous and unsure of himself." Fortunately, that employee was able to suggest that the hiring manager interview the student one more time. (It is very unusual to get such a second chance.) Both faculty and the referring employee coached the applicant on how to present a calm demeanor and on the second interview he did very well and was able to get an offer.

Preparing your stories

For each internship or previous job you've held, be prepared to explain the skill set you have developed. It is important for the interviewer to be able to see that your past experiences have prepared you for the open position. Though the experiences might not be directly relatable to the position, the story you share of how those skills developed and how you will apply them in the new position can be one of the most important things you do. Remember, always connect your story to the position description. While formulating your past internship or work experiences, organize your experiences into the following segments:

1) Ten key experiences and how they relate to the open position
2) Unique characteristics learned, developed or demonstrated through these experiences
3) Transferability of your skills developed to the position

The ten stories of your life and how they relate to the open position:

In preparing for your interview the first step is to formulate your past experiences into stories you are able to tell in the situational interview. These stories will demonstrate qualities that will be viewed as assets to an organization. Your ten stories should be outlined around these following qualities or experiences:

1) Initiative led in the workplace or classroom
2) Tenacity when facing a challenging situation
3) Communication and persuasion
4) Your ability to handle a mistake
5) Your ability to manage and learn from rejection
6) A leadership role you've taken and what you've learned from it
7) An example of helping others
8) A time when you faced an ethical decision and how you handled it
9) A display of your energy, and ability to work through tough problems
10) An example of your flexibility with regards to thought, process or geographical location

Those ten characteristics will be very important stories for the interviewing team and will help you progress to the next step or land a position. For a little context, we will briefly dive into each story, and why they matter to the interviewing team:

1. Initiative in the workplace or classroom
    o Demonstrates that you think "outside the box" and look to improve situations. This also demonstrates leadership in an environment of peers.
2. Tenacity when facing a challenging situation
    o Demonstrates you won't back down from a challenge. You are prepared to work hard, even when the task is difficult.
3. Communication and persuasion
    o You are able to communicate with your team, and persuade those working with you. This demonstrates your interpersonal skills and your ability to become a leader with the company.
4. Your ability to handle a mistake
    o Everyone makes mistakes. Companies look for those who can handle early mistakes and learn from them, not wallow in them.
5. Your ability to manage and learn from rejection
    o Everyone faces rejection. Being able to bounce back (and learn

from) a rejection speaks to one's character.

6. <u>A leadership role you've taken and what you've learned from it</u>
   - o Companies want to develop their new hires into leaders. It is important to show them your aptitude for leadership, and how you can translate past leadership roles into experience to call upon in the workplace.

7. <u>An example of helping others</u>
   - o Every company wants a teammate that is dedicated to helping others. They don't want a team filled with self-dedicated employees; they want employees with a "team-first" mentality.

8. <u>A time when you faced an ethical decision and how you handled it</u>
   - o Everyone has faced an ethical decision. In business, you may face ethical decisions that could put both you and the company at risk. The company will want to know how you handle these types of situations.

9. <u>A display of energy</u>
   - o Companies want new employees with a lot of energy and perseverance. Being able to demonstrate when you were able to work through a tough problem or stayed up all night working will be an advantage in your interview. Though it may seem abstract,

companies want young employees with a lot of energy in the workplace.

10. Your ability to be flexible, both in thought and in location
    o Flexibility is key for new employees in the workforce. There are two principal aspects of flexibility that will be sought after in the interview. Flexibility of mindset and skillset means that you will try new tasks, consider new ideas and be open to new processes. Companies look to their new employees, those who haven't been exposed to many years of workforce practices, to be flexible and try to disrupt the traditional model. Secondly, it will be an advantage if you can explain that you are flexible in hours, location and team. This demonstrates that you will be open to new positions and experiences as they arrive.

In further depth: How to handle the "ethical" question:

One of our students was interviewing with a major automotive manufacturer and was asked a question about ethics. The question was very direct and perhaps even abrasive. "Tell us about a time when you had to compromise your ethics?" The student was equally direct coming back at the interviewers. "I have been raised by parents who taught me right and wrong. My friends understand right and wrong. I have studied the ethical dilemmas that some companies have faced. I have never had a situation where I had to compromise my ethics." Keep your answer simple and be direct. We had another interview situation where the candidate was asked how he would explain a certain issue to businesspeople from another country with whom he would be doing business. The candidate said, "Well, I would tell them what they want to hear!" That answer disqualified the candidate as the interviewers were looking for an answer that indicated how the applicant would handle the situation, not that he would compromise his own viewpoint to simply please a customer.

Insider's tip, the value of flexibility:
   One of our graduates was interviewing for a great position in New York City. At the interview, the interviewer asked, "Do you think you could prepare a weekly report from a macro-economic perspective?" Our candidate answered, "Well, I am not an economist, but as a lawyer, I know how to build a case and I am sure I could do it. It will be a challenge, but I am sure it will be fun." The interviewer replied, "That's what we like to hear!" **Always be positive** and try to display flexibility in your responses.
   In some particular industries, for example logistics, you may be expected to work the graveyard shift. This is part of what the employers feel you need to do to understand all aspects of the process. Try to be equally flexible about assignments that take you away

from home. You may have a preference for a certain region, but to maximize your hiring possibilities, make sure you appear open and flexible. Recognize that some major companies are expecting to lose top candidates from the West Coast, just because they are less desirable location. Your geographic flexibility can land you the job!

The importance of working in teams:

Most jobs will require you to spend the majority of your day in small teams. During application review and interview, companies will look for specific examples of how you work with teams. Be able to highlight these both on your resume and in your interview answers. Most importantly, be able to bring up any leadership roles you've had directing small teams.

It is an added bonus to explain how you have worked on or led **diverse teams**. Many students have worked on teams with the same types of people (sports, Greek life, etc.), but very few have had experiences working and leading diverse teams. Diverse teams can consist of teammates of different backgrounds, skillsets, expectations or goals. At work you will have individuals with widely varying skillsets and perspectives driven by their functional roles and levels, e.g. accounting or human resources, vice president or analyst. Being able to demonstrate your contribution and leadership in a diverse environment will allow the interviewer to see how these experiences are directly related to teams in their workplace.

These examples may come from classroom projects and team assignments.

As a freshman or sophomore, remember to keep track of the experiences you've had working on teams. Write down your experiences, teammates, and results. It will be important to call upon these experiences in your application process and can sometimes be easily forgotten.

Know the company's technology:

At technology-based companies, the most effective business analysts are those that understand the basics of the technology. Often, in interviews, tech companies will ask their business hires to explain a bit about their products and the market in general. Be prepared for this while conducting your research. If you are able to take a few elective classes related to a certain industry, this will help immensely in your application.

Know the technology, but also the strategy!

A common interview question: *"What do you think is the next strategic step or shift for our organization?"* Your answer will allow the interviewer to see that you have a good grasp of the major trends and that you are intelligent enough to understand how macro factors affect a specific company. Understanding the industry in depth is unusual for a new hire and a sure way you can demonstrate your preparation.

Interview example:

When interviewing for an information services company, Tucker was asked, "What do you think might be the next step for our company to find a new market?" This question requires you to be analytical and understand both the evolving economy and the product. When preparing for the interview, research where the product now stands in its market and how the company is going to continue to expand and find **market growth**. In his preparations, Tucker had read in their annual reports' *Management Discussion and Analysis* section that they were looking to expand their news services to major universities across the country. He explained that he'd read about their proposed market entrance strategy and said he agreed with the approach but saw additional growth opportunities for to integrating their services into law firms and major financial institutions. By demonstrating that he had read their annual report and that he was able to complement their strategy with another avenue for growth, Tucker showed that he had done his homework and had thought about their growth strategies. This is what really matters. Most interviewers will not fault your logical answer, even if they disagree, but they want to see that you have invested thought into their situation. Doing this will differentiate you from most applicants. You don't need an in-depth knowledge of all trends of the technologies, but you do need basic understanding and the ability to talk about pertinent issues. When entering an interview, be able to understand why they're **growing or**

losing market share, and how can they create additional growth.

Application example:
Let's pretend you are entering an interview with an information security company, Company X. By doing some research you can see that a strategic change that is facing the industry today is that Company X is finding they are under-protected against the threat of a cyber attack. By reading about the marketplace, you can see that other firms in the industry have increased their acquisitions to address the lack of internal talent. It would be advantageous to understand the topic and demonstrate your knowledge during an interview. By presenting that you understand that the industry is going through a change and that you are interested in gaining more knowledge in the subject, you prove two things to the recruiters:

- You have the knowledge to understand the skills that are important to the position
- You have taken the time and put in the effort to research current trends in the industry

During an interview, the way you carry yourself, the actions you take, your tone of voice and the stories you tell will all be points of focus and critique by the interviewer. Aside from the initial story, the interviewers will key into your ability to follow their answer format instructions and will observe nonverbal details such as posture, expression and focus. You are judged not only on the answers you provide, but the entire experience you give the interviewer.

Etiquette and Professionalism

Your dress and body language matter:
Personal appearance is a major criterion being scored during the interview. When preparing for an interview and choosing your dress, be cautious and aware of the organizational culture, and how the interview team is likely to dress. Though you want to **match the dress of the culture**, err on the side of conservatism and ***never* be underdressed**. If you are interviewing for a Fortune 500, men should dress in a suit and women a pantsuit. When picking colors, be conservative. Black, gray or dark blue suit with a white or blue shirt is recommended. Ties can be slightly more colorful but don't be over the top. Black ties are discouraged. If you expect the setting to be much less formal, a suit without a tie is a good option for men. Interviewees who show up in jeans or casual clothing are **placing themselves at an extreme disadvantage**. Dressing properly shows respect to the organization.

How to dress for a phone interview:
In the phone interview be sure the area you are working in is clean and uncluttered and that you are the same. The way you are dressed will impact how you respond and answer

questions. Our top-performing young managers all, without any exceptions, recommend that you dress appropriately for even the phone interview. Dress casually, but be clean and polished. Also, be especially aware of your dress during Skype interviews. We know of an interviewer who asked the candidate to go over to a counter that he could see and pick up a pen that was lying there. The candidate was forced to stand up to do so and the interviewer immediately saw that the candidate was in his underwear. Not a great impression, to say the least!

No cell phones!
Though it really should go without saying, remember to turn your phone off and stow it away during an interview. Having your cell phone ring, or, worse, looking at your phone during an interview is a sign of extreme disrespect and will certainly count against you during your interview.

Body language:
In addition to dress, body language and energy are judged during an interview. You want to appear engaged, energetic and alert by leaning forward during an interview, using (occasionally) your hands to talk, and keeping eye contact with the interviewers. Do not slouch, cross your arms or look down at the table when speaking with the panel. Sit forward in your chair and sit straight up. At the beginning and the end of the interview, give a firm handshake. Never prop up your head with your hands and no hands in your face during

an interview! Be aware that a great interview can often be ruined by bad posture and body language, so don't get too comfortable!

The introductions and first few questions

Introductions:
Though there isn't much time allocated to the meet and greet prior to the interview, this introduction sets the tone for the rest of the meeting. The saying, "people judge you within the first three minutes of meeting you," is indeed *true* in interviewing, so there are a few things of which you must be aware:

The interview isn't only conducted in the conference room:
Note that the interview begins the moment you step onto the company's facilities and doesn't end until the moment you leave. Everyone you meet, particularly receptionists and office assistants, is important to treat with absolute respect. If you arrive and disrespect the person working at the front door, this will likely be passed back to the hiring managers. How you treat the lower tiers within an organization demonstrates a lot about your character. They are watching how you treat everyone in the office and how you conduct yourself outside of the interview room.

Greeting and first few minutes in the office:
While greeting the team, shake hands, smile, look them in the eye and be appreciative for the opportunity. It is important to let them make the first move whether it be moving to a

conference room, getting coffee or getting started. You are a guest on their time and you want to go along with their schedule and their tone. Make sure not to pander, but if warranted, give compliments about the work area and the city, as it is important to seem impressed.

If they offer you water or coffee, **say yes**. This may sound quirky, but saying "no" can imply that you are nervous or that you are expecting to leave quickly. If you move to a conference room to start the interview, don't immediately jump into "interview mode." Keep the casual dialogue going as long as possible and casually transition into your semi-serious mentality during the interview. The person interviewing you would also like to keep it as casual as it allows them to see what you're like as a person.

The following are common extensions of the traditional interview:

- **Ride-alongs**: Additionally, many sales teams will require candidates to join a "ride-along" as they visit their districts and customers. This can be more important than the "in-office" interview. These experiences are often more relaxed and each party can see if they identify with the cultural fit of the organization. If you are interviewing for a sales job, understand that the "ride-along" may be a portion of your interview and everything you say and do may be reported back to the decision makers.

- **Going to lunch**: Eating lunch will give the company the ability to evaluate you in a professional setting, so be cognizant that it is really a continuation of the interview. If you go to lunch with an interviewing manager, we recommend:
  - Let the manager indicate where you should sit
  - Don't order alcohol
  - Don't order something that will easily spill
  - Don't order the most expensive thing on the menu

Sitting to your advantage:
The seat you take at an interview table can change the dynamic and potentially the outcome of the interview. When entering a room, allow the host to guide you to a seat, but if the choice is left to you, try to face as many people as possible in the room. Avoid sitting between two people, as it can be awkward to look back and forth, and you will inevitably favor one over another. Sit facing the panel, allowing yourself to address all parties at once.

Common introduction questions:
1) Tell me a little bit about yourself
2) Walk me through your resume
3) Why do you want to work with our company?
4) Why this position?
5) Why this industry?
6) What are your greatest strengths/weaknesses?

7) Where else have you applied and been interviewing?

Asked about your interviews with other companies?
No matter what, always be honest in an interview. The question of your progress with other companies will likely come up and, if answered correctly, can work to your advantage. If you're interviewing with other notable name-brand companies, or more specifically, a competitor in their industry, this will hint to the interviewer that others have recognized you as a talent and may extend you an offer. This may intrigue them to better consider your application and work quickly to capture your talent before their competition does. It would be highly unusual for an interviewer to pursue extensive questioning about your other interviews, however a basic timeline of where you are in the process with other companies may be asked.

The Elevator Pitch

Most interviews open with one simple question that will set the tone of the rest of your interview: "**Tell me a little bit about yourself**" or "**walk me through your resume.**"

Tell me about yourself is different from walk me through your resume:
Telling someone about yourself should be exactly what it sounds like. Where are you from? What do you do outside of the

classroom? This should not be a completely unstructured answer, but it is important to share some more personal information that allows the interviewer to understand what is important in your life and how have you been shaped by your interests and past.

"Walk me through your resume"....where to begin?

In our opinion, this is the perfect question for any sales position. You know more about yourself than anyone else. You are your own brand and you have to find a way to highlight your experiences in a way that will make you attractive to the interviewer.

First, make sure that you **do not ramble**. Keep this answer to a one-minute sales pitch where you are selling your product (yourself) for the requisition. We want to stress that you need to be very careful not to run on with your answer. Generally, we stress that all answers, regardless of question, should not run over ninety seconds.

Fill out the boxes below:

I am: I am from: I am graduating from: I studied:	I had the opportunity to: 1) Internship 2) Internship/club 3) Volunteer activity	I am here today because:

Example introductory paragraph for "walk me through your resume":

My name is _____ and I am graduating in _____ of _____ with a degree in _____ and a minor in _____ from the University of _____. I am from _____. During my time at university I had the opportunity to participate in

_____,
_____ and
_____. This summer I held _____ internship/position. Through my internship/full-time experience, I've developed _____, _____ and _____ skills. I am here today because I am particularly interested in the _____ position and I am impressed by your organization. I am

_____, _____ and extremely hard-working and really hope for the opportunity to start my career with

_____.

What skills should I mention in my elevator pitch?

Be truthful about the skills you've developed, but if possible, focus on the skills and qualities that are highlighted in the requisition. If there weren't skills listed, think which skills of yours might be most relevant to that specific requisition.

The most important question you will be asked: "Why do you want to work for our company?"

Brief exercise: Pick the company you would most like to work with. Now, in 60 seconds, explain: Why you want to work there? Bring a balanced approach. Why that specific company and **how does its culture complement your work style**? What about this company puts it above the rest in your mind? Why does this industry interest you? These are all points to tie into your 60-second answer. Remember, be as specific as possible and avoid generalities when speaking about why you're interested and why you fit. Since you will have carefully prepared you should be able to demonstrate knowledge of the company and the business unit for which you will be interviewing.

Example:

Software Company X: I am seeking this job with your organization because I feel the position presents a perfect combination of my interests and my strengths. I am a student of financial analysis and love solving problems. Through my internships in an adjacent industry, I have developed a skill-set that prepares me for a career with your division. I have always been a believer in your philosophy of open source software and know it is the trend of the future. I am particularly excited about your recent product line, the Widget 1000, as I believe you have found a niche in the marketplace, and provide a fantastic user experience. I have strong quantitative abilities which I believe will complement your company culture. This job is well-suited to me and I am very excited to start my career with your company. I really want this opportunity.

The goal is to talk a little bit about yourself, but also **a little bit about the company.** Without being obsessive or obnoxious, show enough interest in the organization to make the host feel proud to work there.

Situational Questions

Many Fortune 500 companies are increasingly using situational/behavioral questions to understand your skill sets for areas they see as most applicable to the position. The situational interview questions will take the majority of the time during your session. Typically, there will be five to ten questions requiring a multi-pronged answer. Though situational questions will differ, the response structure you follow will largely stay the same. It can be broken out into four sections, each equally important. Please note: situational questions are looking for **specific examples**. Do not speak in generalities – the interviewing team wants to hear a specific example from your past. Additionally, to make sure you hit all three points of the answer, the interviewers will sometimes break their paper into three sections, noting your input for each of the STAR columns.

STAR format overview

1. Specific **S**ituation/**T**ask
2. Specific **A**ction
3. Specific **R**esult
4. What you learned

The primary objectives the company seeks to learn from using the STAR format:

Situation & Task: The interviewers will look for you to build the background of the story. It is important to give them context of your actions, and explain who was involved in the situation.

Action: What did you do? Specifically explain what you did as opposed to the others that you worked with. Explain how big the action was, and who was involved.

Result: What was the result of your action? Did the team finish the project? Did the club increase its funding by 50%? Outline in detail the results of what you specifically did and quantify the result, if possible. Very importantly, explain what would have been the result if you had not have been involved.

What you learned: What key takeaways came of this action? Did it open your perspective? How can you leverage this experience into your future workplace? Explain in detail what you took away from this experience, and how it helped you develop your skill-set or abilities.

It's OK to ask follow-up questions:

The interviewers will not mind if you take light hand-written notes during the interview process. It is also OK to feedback your understanding of the question during an interview. Be polite in stating that "I believe the question you're asking is…" and it is **OK to ask the question** again if you feel that it wasn't perfectly clear or you simply didn't understand it. (Please limit yourself to one to two of these requests in an hour interview.)

How do you demonstrate multiple points in a single question response?

Example Question: *"Tell me about a time when you had to change the way something was done."*
Answer: In my first internship at a clothing manufacturer while working in their quality control department, I was given the task of tracking orders. My initial attempt was to code all the orders by number, but after the first three submittals, I realized that my method was only completing at an efficiency of 75%. I analyzed the situation and asked those employees around me for their recommendations. After evaluating the situation and speaking with co-workers I developed a color-coded systems of tracking orders. After applying this method, the efficiency moved to 95%. Getting the opinions of others reinforced the positive results driven from collaboration.

With this brief answer, **you are telling the interviewer the following**:

1) Most fundamentally, you are able to answer the question in the correct way by using the STAR method (you can follow directions.)
2) You make mistakes (you're honest), understand your mistakes, communicate your mistakes and learn from them
3) You communicate with others
4) You find it important to address problems and identify a solution
5) You see your mistakes as learning opportunities
6) You are constantly striving to improve a situation or a process

One Question? Three to five opportunities!
As we demonstrate above, being able to tie in **three to five positive points per question** requires immense preparation. You have between 20-45 minutes to sell yourself, so we recommend that you use each question to demonstrate more than one personal quality about yourself. There are typically five to seven major situational questions posed in an interview. What this means is that for each one question, if you deliver *three to five positive personal qualities* as demonstrated by the sample answer above, you can highlight 25-35 qualities about yourself over the life of the interview

A reminder word of caution: while answering behavioral questions, be sure **not to speak in generalities** but rather give them the full detail of every step in the process. The interviewers will be looking for the details in your thought process and your actions taken after addressing the problem or issue. If you speak generally, they will often ask follow-up questions (negatively impacting your score) to get you to further explain the details in the process. As stated before, the interview panel will likely be more interested in observing your thought process than the actual answer.

Note: It is fine, and even encouraged to explicitly explain the skills you've demonstrated after telling a relatable story. Sometimes you may want to end your structured interview question with words such as: *"Through this experience I demonstrated leadership and communication and improved my understanding of how a small group operates."* It's unnecessary to force those words into the answer, but if it wasn't clear through your story, it will be helpful to specifically explain your achievements.

The two most important accomplishments to highlight in an interview:
    In an interview when touching on your past experiences, there are two aspects that the interviewer will be looking for, above all else:

1. **Did you go above and beyond what was required of you?**

2. Did you improve a process resulting in saved time/money?

Particularly when joining older generations in the workplace, they often look to recent graduates as the tech-savvy innovative thinkers with *an eye for process improvement*. Being able to demonstrate that you improved upon a process at work, whether it be a Microsoft Excel-related issue, or improving a strategy at a call bank, interviewers see this as the highest form of thinking and will consider process improvements as a key asset when evaluating you.

Speak in percentages:

When communicating the process improvements you've made, speak in percentages. It might not sound like much if you saved your small company $10,500, but if it is explained as saving the company 5% of its budget, it becomes a more significant accomplishment.

Non-traditional interview structures and questions:

Some questions will be abstract, be prepared!

Some companies, primarily tech, consulting and investment management will ask abstract questions to understand your thought process. Though one cannot prepare answers for these types of questions, be aware that they may be presented.

168

Insider tip: One of our students was interviewing with a major investment house for an analyst position. After the introductory questions, he was asked a number of statistics and probability questions. The questions ranged from population questions to odds in baseball games. Though he was not prepared for these types of questions, his quantitative edge allowed him to answer sufficiently. Be prepared for abstract math questions in finance-based interviews.

Insider tip: We know of a certain western governor who was interviewing a candidate for a staff position. The governor pointed to a huge crystal ashtray at the center of the conference room table. "Tell me about that ashtray," the governor boomed! The candidate looked the governor right in the eye and said, "Governor, I didn't come here to talk about crystal ashtrays, I came here to discuss my candidacy for X." The candidate jumped right in, explaining in his 45-second elevator pitch, why he was the right person and the best candidate. Ultimately he got the job!

Explaining the steps in your thought process is important:
Many interview techniques are designed to expose the interviewers to your thought process. Questions will revolve around solving a complex problem, step-by-step, allowing you to walk the team through your thinking. In these types of interview scenarios, be aware of the need to explain clearly how you worked

from one point to the next, providing insight into how you solve problems. Be very methodical and explain all the angles and nuances of your thinking. Sometimes, the interviewer will even ask you to break down your explanation to the most fundamental level, as if you were explaining a process to a child.

How to close the interview

Leaving a lasting image with the interviewer is invaluable. Regardless of how the interview felt, it is important to **drive home one last message** and be strong in your closing pitch. The closing message should be one final conclusion of how your strengths and goals meet with the opportunity presented. In closing an interview, regardless of how it went, one should always end with this closing pitch, or one like it:

As I see this opportunity, I see a job that has a unique opportunity to combine my interests and my strengths. My strengths being

_____, _____,
_____. And my interests being
_____,_____. I can promise you that no one will work harder or want to succeed more than me. I am fascinated by what your company does, eager to work hard, and I am confident that overtime I can succeed in your organization. **I really, really want this job.**"

When closing the interview, demonstrate **passion, determination and strong will**. If you are able to clearly demonstrate these characteristics at the close of your interview, your enthusiasm will stick with the panel and will stay in their minds throughout the evaluation process. Though it sounds fundamental, vocalize that **you want this job**. You will be surprised how many students go through interviews, and never say the words, **"I really want this job."**

Practice your sales pitch:

Sell yourself. Practice in front of the mirror and be truly confident in what you are saying. Regardless of any possible difficulties during the interview, you will be surprised that a question with which you struggled can be mitigated with a successful closing speech. Believing in oneself and having strong self-confidence is contagious and most definitely something people want in a teammate. Be sure you master your closing speech.

Note that many career services departments and many business departments will have facilities that allow you to be taped throughout the practice interview process.

Exit timelines should be avoided:

The interviewers, particularly as you advance in the process, are looking not only at what you can do in the position for which you have applied, but in terms of the potential you are bringing to the company. They are evaluating whether they perceive you could, with time, move up the company's management ranks. If you are hired, a lot of time and energy will have gone into the process to recruit you, and a lot of time, money and energy will go into training and mentoring you in your first position. Therefore, you need to be very careful not to introduce any negative variables into the conversation that might indicate you will be with the company for just a couple of years. How could anyone get this impression? Here's an example:

We had a student whose long-term goal was to become a lawyer. He was asked what he saw himself doing when he was 35. He made the mistake of answering that he one day wants to be involved with criminal law, and hoped to attend a major law school in the near future. This career path had absolutely nothing to do with the corporation where he was interviewing. Our advice is that fifteen years is a long time from today, and that while answering honestly is important, think through the possibilities and only share the ones that pertain to the job and company for which you have applied.

If your family owns a business, don't give the interviewers any indication that you plan to return to the family business in the near future.

Asked about an MBA?

If asked about an MBA or advanced degrees, we suggest you answer with the following: "I may want to return to graduate school at some point, particularly if your company feels its important to advance my career with a masters degree. In a perfect world, I would like to remain with the company and pursue the advanced degree over several years. I would want to have a lot of experience with the company before I started thinking about graduate studies."

It should be noted that the average age of the top full-time MBA programs is about 27, as good schools are looking for students with four to six years of meaningful work experience.

Questions to ask the interviewer during an interview:

In the final minutes of the interview, the panel will open the floor for you to ask questions about the position, the team and the company. This may be the only truly open, non-structured dialogue during the interview, so this portion is greatly important. This is **your time to interview them**. Use your time wisely. It is best to prepare three to five questions that are intelligent and reveal something positive about yourself in addition to assisting you in learning more about the position. Though it is an open conversation, **don't ask anything you can find online**! If there is a panel, it is recommended that you address a range of interviewers during your question time and don't focus exclusively on one individual. The questions are an opportunity to learn more about the position but also a time to **showcase your intelligence**.

Some specific examples of questions to ask your panel:

- What is something that I could do in the next several months that will better prepare me for when I could potentially start in the summer?

- Will I have a chance to meet my supervisor before I start?

    o This is very important to clarify if they are not present for the interview day

- Can you recommend any books or articles that will better help me prepare for the position?

- What is a typical next role for people who perform well in this role? What is a typical career pathway?

- If you were just graduating college in my position, why would you choose to come work for your company?
    o This will drive home the fact that you are interviewing them while they are interviewing you. You have options and you are valuable and want to be sold on the company. (Be sensitive in the way you phrase this answer!)

- What is the next step in this process? (If not explained, this is a must ask)!

Direct specific questions to different people on the panel:

During your question and answer time it is important to focus on individuals through your questions rather than just openly addressing the whole group. One of Tucker's interviews with a major retail company included an analyst currently serving in the position for which he was interviewing. Tucker was able to address this person (rather than her manager) and ask her what she would do to prepare for the position if she had six more months in school, as he did at the time. The analyst would likely be able to give Tucker the most detailed plan, as she was currently serving in the role. By asking her, Tucker demonstrated that he **valued her opinion** just as much as one of the senior managers in the room. She responded by saying she would have audited another accounting class, as the first few months can be accounting-intensive, and additionally suggested he brush up on the information systems software that they were currently using. Tucker gained valuable insight while also showing respect to the least senior person in the room.

Investigate how your potential boss is regarded within the company:

Though you should never directly ask, pay attention to the manner in which others refer to your potential managers. Your direct manager will have significant influence on your experience in your first few years. Keep note if they are well-positioned within the company, or if they are spoken poorly about within the organization – this will be important for your career development!

What happens after an interview?

Meet the team!

During the interview day, make an effort to introduce yourself to as many people as possible. Meeting a greater number of people increases your chances of making personal connections and receiving a recommendation from the "inside."

Insider Tip: When Tucker interviewed with an information services company in San Francisco he felt that it went decently well. After the interview Tucker asked, "*Can I sit with an analyst* who is currently doing the job I am applying for?" This showed that he was interested in taking additional time to sit and meet with the members of the groups. Also, it allowed Tucker to **develop another point of contact** within the company.

He was placed with one of the first-year analysts. Tucker sat with her for 20-30 minutes and was able to strike up a good relationship. He was able to explain to her his interest in the position (though not as thoroughly as in the interview.) After he returned home, he sent his newly-developed contact an email restating his interest and sending his appreciation for her time. She wrote back that she would "put in a good word for [him] with the hiring manager." Tucker had turned a 20-minute conversation with a lower-level employee into an inside recommendation!

The advantage of having a recommendation come from inside the team, in that exact position for which you are interviewing, is that those who have sent the support know exactly what they are looking for in a teammate. Those who you sit with won't know your resume or your past experience - all they have is their personal judgment of how well you would fit on the team. Remember, follow up with any and all contacts and restate your interest in the position.

Meeting more of the team allows you to understand the company culture:
As we discussed earlier, it is paramount to understand the culture within an organization. Knowing that you will spend between 40-100 hours weekly in this environment highlights the importance of being comfortable with your co-workers and with the company culture. The culture within an organization is often driven from the top; but it can vary widely from company to company, industry to industry and even within different divisions or units of a company. Some cultures work long, strict hours while some work in an ad hoc, flexible environment. Some companies honor seniority while others value "groupthink," where key contributions come from all ranks of the organization. Company culture is an important intangible to recognize and should certainly carry weight when selecting an organization. Though you don't need to be identical in personality to everyone in the organization, it is important to find a company with like-minded individuals.

A tip regarding receptions:

The strict situational awareness doesn't end with the interview. Often, applicants are invited to receptions or dinners during the interview process. If alcohol is served, **stay away from it**. The company is watching how you perform in a social setting and you don't want to involve any unpredictable variables that might influence your personality or demeanor. It is perfectly acceptable to simply have a soda at an event.

The required work after the application submittal

Though many might argue that your time is best filled by more applications after you've gone through a first round of interviews, there are a few tactics to add value to your applications and prepare you for the next step in the process. Typically, **organizations take a few weeks** to get back to you with answers, and the larger the organization, the longer the process, (yet some Fortune 100s get back to an interviewer in one to two days depending on the urgency to fill an application spot). In this time in limbo, there are many steps to take to prepare you for the next phase in the process. Your primary responsibilities include:

- Alerting all references that you have provided their names and giving them all the necessary information for a potential call from the organization

- Developing Excel and other Microsoft-based skills
- Further interview/presentation practice

Alerting References:

References may be caught off-guard if they receive a call without warning and won't be able to provide the organization with an effective recommendation. A poor, awkward or off-point recommendation will significantly hurt your candidacy. It is common courtesy to let a reference know beforehand that you've used them as a point of contact and that you appreciate their support. After finishing your first interview, be sure to immediately alert all references and let them know that you are in consideration for a position and that they may be getting a call from the company. Tell them how the process has gone thus far and what the next steps are. When you alert them, re-send them your resume, and explain the company and the position. Additionally, update your references on any recent developments with your applications.

If planning on using a reference in an application, it is necessary to first **get their permission** to do so. If you're planning on indicating to the company that you have an internal contact, be sure that the contact is aware, and OK with you submitting their name. Additionally, by letting them know you're going to use their name in your application package, they may likely have advice for your approach to this submittal!

Excel and Information Systems training:
In one final interview, Tucker was asked to explain some advanced functions required in creating databases. He explained that he had not had much training in advanced SQL functions but that he was planning on taking a class before he graduated to prepare for the database-focused work. Your ability to quickly learn how to run reports and analyze data is an excellent way that you can add value to an organization. If possible, be able to demonstrate in the interview the training and comfort you have with Excel.

We recommend visiting your university's computer center for direction on Excel training. If classes are not offered at your university, there are a number of online resources that can teach you the basics. The first place to look is Microsoft's website for any free seminars in Excel 2003 and 2007. If you are able to pay $100-$200 there are a number of online resources that will complement your free online training.

Fine-tune your interview skills:
During your downtime during the process, continue to practice your interview presentation skills. Continue to tweak and perfect your "about me" statement or your closing pitch. These types of questions will surely arise in all types of interviews, and they are questions for which you can practice your delivery and message. As we have touched on before, "Tell me a little bit about yourself" is the most important question that you will face in an interview. Practice your delivery, timing and

overall message. When you're walking between classes, say your delivery out loud, deliver it to friends and family; this question can make or break an interview and you can be certain that it will be asked.

Company-provided problem sets:

Companies will sometimes send you problem statements to work through before (or after) you proceed on in an interview. Students will receive a problem set with questions relating to the position for which they are interviewing. For example, if it's a corporate finance role, companies may send an accounting problem statement and request it be sent back within 48 hours. An applicant for a role in operations may receive a case study about increasing factory efficiency and will need to provide their written answer or explain their approach during an upcoming interview. Companies aren't specifically looking for one answer over another. They are interested in your **thought process** that you walk them through. It is important to complete these problems honestly without any outside help, as it will likely be the type of work you'll be expected to handle!

Personality Tests:

Companies may provide personality tests for you to take during the interview process. These personality tests will give another indication as to whether or not you are a good fit with the organization. Don't think that companies are looking for only a particular personality type. Companies need all types of personalities for a diverse workforce – just be yourself!

Take a free Myers-Briggs Type Indicator assessment:
Companies may be interested in understanding your Myers-Briggs assessment. Regardless of if it is requested in an application period, we recommend you take this free online test for your own records. The test will tell you your personality type and how well you associate with others of similar or different personality types. It might be an interesting data point to bring up somewhere along the interview process.

Keep the data on your interviews!
After your interview, successful or not, replay the interview from start to finish in your head and write down all the questions and your answers. Though the interview is over, it is important to create a repository of questions and answers to prepare yourself for any following interviews. By writing down all your questions and answers you will be able to evaluate where you can improve and prepare yourself for follow-on interviews with the same company or others. Recording this data is valuable for self-analysis and fine-tuning your answers.

How to stay in the minds of the interviewers:
After your interview, your main goal should be to stay in the interviewer's heads. **Be persistent without being pesky**. As

previously stated, to show your intent on moving forward in the process, an important question is: "What is the next step in the process?" Most likely, they will explain that you will hear back within one to two weeks. During this period, you need to keep yourself in their mind. Keep the names of everyone you had contact with while you going through the process, and build an ***Excel spreadsheet tracking your contacts within the organization,*** *as we've discussed before.* Take their business cards, and the day following your interview, send a thank-you email and restate your interest in the position. Don't wait, as the team may be meeting early the next morning to decide upon your candidacy. **Note:** for some sales jobs, post-interview follow-up is a point of scoring on your application.

Sample follow-up email:

Dear Susan,

Thank you for taking the time to facilitate my interview yesterday. I was extremely impressed with your organization and the team mentality demonstrated by your group. I believe that I have unique strengths that will add great value to your organization if given the opportunity. If there is anything else you should need from me going forward in this process, please let me know. I am very excited for the opportunity.

Thank you for your time,
Johnny Jobseeker

By following up with the interviewers and everyone else you had the opportunity to meet, you are showing them that you are serious about the position, have the initiative to follow up, and have taken every opportunity to re-enforce your qualifications for the position. The interviewers will usually share their notes with each other, so don't send them all the same stock email!

If you meet a more senior person during your interview experience, be sure to send them a note. In your note include the line: ***"This is an opportunity that I really want."*** Thanking a more senior member of the staff may result in them circulating your email back to the human resources department. This will certainly have a positive impact on your application.

Haven't heard back in over two weeks?

If you haven't heard from a company for over two weeks after your interview, it is fine, and even encouraged, to send your contact within human resources a follow-up email inquiring about the status of your application. Don't be pesky, but being interested in the next step is an important sign of your seriousness to the interviewing team.

Section IV in review:

In section IV we covered the different interview structures and questions you may face in different types of interviews. We went over how to network oneself into an organization and established outlines for the opening and closing of interviews. In the next section, we go over your actions and responsibilities after your interview. Remember, the search isn't complete after the interview; it's complete after your final steps with an offer in hand - next we will dive into the final leg of the journey.

Sample interview questions for your practice

Personal or Past Experience:
1) Tell me a little bit about yourself.
2) Why are you here today?
3) Why didn't you take a job with _____?
4) What was your favorite class in school?
5) Why did you leave the company where you interned?
6) What do you like to do outside of your schoolwork?
7) Where do you want to be in five years?
8) Why did you choose your college major?
9) Did you go abroad and why/where did you go?
10) How long do you plan to stay with our company?
11) Are you used to stressful work environments?
12) What type of hours would you expect to work?
13) How would your friends describe your personality type?
14) Do you want to get your graduate degree? When? What degree?

15) What's your greatest strength?
16) What's your greatest weakness?
17) Who else are you interviewing with?
18) What class was most difficult for you?
19) What's the most important thing you learned through _____ internship?
20) What did you like/dislike about your college?
21) Do you speak other languages? And if you don't, why not?
22) What are you the most proud of that isn't on your resume?
23) Can you explain your leadership style?
24) How did you pick your college?
25) How would you describe your personality?
26) What's a big decision that you've recently made and how did you weigh your options?
27) What's the trait you respect most in a person?
28) What kind of managers do you work well/not work well with?
29) What salary do you expect?

Situational or Structured:
Tell me about a time when you...
1) went against a group effort
2) had to stand-up for what was right
3) showed leadership
4) had to work under deadline
5) showed initiative on a project
6) had difficulty resolving a dispute in your group

Company Knowledge:
1) Why our company?
2) How would you improve our webpage or what do you think about our mission statement?
3) Tell us about our competitors and what they do well.
4) Can you tell me a little bit about our products?
5) What kind of company do you want to work for in 5 years?
6) Can you tell us about our company leadership?
7) Do you see yourself wanting to go into management or become a specialist?
8) Why do you want to start your career here and not with a larger (or smaller) organization?
9) Where do you think we'll find growth in this market?

General Intelligence / Other:
1) What's the last book you've read?
2) How would you describe today's macro economy?
3) What do you think will happen in X country, or a specific region?
4) How familiar are you with Excel? Can you explain a macro?
5) Are you comfortable with the Office suite?
6) Who's your favorite business or social leader and why?
7) Name a company you really admire. Why?
8) What stock would you recommend?

9) Can you explain to us the financial crisis of 2009?
10) Why would -- or wouldn't -- you buy our stock?

Section V: Post Offer

Congratulations! You've successfully landed one or multiple job offers. Now the work begins: Which offer to take? Being young in your career, the first job you take will propel you in a direction, while also it will *prevent* you from immediately exploring other career interests. Realistically, if you have two offers, you can't make both companies happy, but you must decline the company you don't choose on good terms. **Never burn your bridges,** as you might someday need to return.

Most of the time you will find yourself with just one offer. The below sections are designed for you to evaluate if you should take the present offer, or continue your search. Though you may be tempted to take the first and so-far only offer available, be cognizant that as you have made it this far with one company, you can likely land another offer with some additional searching using improved techniques.

Some important questions we address in Section V:
- What work is required of you post-offer?
- What unforeseen variables will affect each company, and how to identify these in your selection?
  - Macro trends – what do they mean for the company?
  - CEO and management structure
- How do you see yourself moving forward from each position?

- What does the total compensation package look like?
- Which position provides you with the best path forward?

No offer? It is all a learning experience!

If you went through the process with no offer, do not be discouraged. It is a fantastic sign of your aptitude that you made it this far in a very competitive process. Your best interviews come after a few practice interviews and now you will be better prepared for the next position.

Though you may want to write the company off forever, there is a lot to be learned from the rejection. What could you have done better? Which sections of the interview were the easiest, which the hardest? Creating a post-interview repository of data that highlights where you may have gone wrong will help you prepare for your success in the next opportunity.

Deciding between two different offers:

If you have two offers but you don't feel that either is close to your perfect job, go back to your two-year goals in Section III, to decide which offer will best suit you moving forward. What goals did you have for yourself before you started the career search? **Which job will put you in the best position to start on a path to accomplish these goals?** Early in your career, you likely don't know what you want and you don't know where your true strengths lie. To find a position that will give

Get to Work
Tucker Stein & Jack Osborn

you the best advantage moving forward, evaluate each offer for the most career flexibility, and the most transferrable skill development. Though it might seem too soon to think of exit options, these questions must drive your decision process in selecting a job.

The following aspects should be considered when choosing between two positions or evaluating if you should take your one present offer:

1) Job Description
2) Company visibility, size and "brand" name
3) Transferable skills which can be acquired
4) Is the industry within your area of interest
5) Location, pay, benefits and regional taxes
6) Company culture (including reputation)
7) Training opportunities before the job starts
8) Exit opportunities
9) Internal promotion path
10) Mentoring or management relationship
11) How well you think you will fit in with the culture

Timeline for acceptance:
Companies will often give you two to three weeks to accept or decline. During these weeks, speak with **as many people as** possible. Call on professors, graduates, family friends to discuss the pros and cons of each position. It is helpful to write out benefits and disadvantages of each job compared to one

another. Though they may not be apparent, and you are relieved to simply have a position, there are disadvantages to taking each job.

Though it might seem impossible to choose between two hypothetical positions, no two offers will be the same and there will often be a clear winner. However, occasionally, one may choose to take a position that could be viewed less favorably by the general public. For instance, we've seen students accept internships over full-time positions because the internship fell directly within their scope of interest while the full-time position seemed distant from their goals and growth opportunities were limited. Most likely, you will have a gut feeling about which offer is best for your future. Once you accept one offer, and professionally decline the other, don't look back.

Another way to outline the comparison of the two companies into the categories that matter the most to you is to create a side-by-side analysis. Though your own top 10 aspects of a career may vary, use the below grid as an example. Again, note that these techniques can be used to evaluate any number of present offers.

	Company X	Company Y
Training		

Pay & benefits		
Location		
Transferable skills		
Exit opportunities		
Promotion path		
Alignment with interests		
Company reputation		
Management relationship		
Work/Life balance		
Grad degree sponsorship		
Company culture		

The advantages of a position won't always be obvious:

One of our exceptional students ultimately took a position in logistics and distribution with a major national company. Several years later, she came back to speak to our students in their Business final seminar. In their critiques of her presentation, while everyone wrote that it was outstanding, several individuals couldn't understand why such an intelligent woman was working "on a loading dock." What these students failed to understand is that this woman had actually turned down several other opportunities, some of which had better starting pay, and took the logistics and distribution position because of its mid- to long-term potential. Today she is an upper-level executive with this firm.

Another very talented student chose not to take a full-time position directly out of college.

Instead, he chose an internship with a national retailer. He understood that if he did well in the six-month internship that he would be offered a full-time position. He really wanted to work in retail management, and this was the doorway through which any applicant for senior management needed to enter. He was very successful and today is employed in that company's fast track management program.

Tucker's Story: Tucker was offered two full-time positions within a week of one another. One position was in an Information Technology conglomerate in a customer service/relations field. The other was with a manufacturing company in a corporate finance role. Though he was extremely interested in technology and information services, Tucker went with the corporate finance opportunity. **Here's why:** as a recent graduate, you should avoid anything that will confine you to limited skills and limited flexibility. The best roles for recent graduates are those that provide you with the greatest flexibility in using and developing skill sets. This should be your goal: gain the **greatest base of experience and knowledge** that will allow you to develop a range of easily adaptable and transferable skills.

Tucker saw two very different positions. One position would provide him with a niche, specialty knowledge, while the other offer would let him experience a number of different positions and expose him to different worlds within finance. The offer that Tucker declined was higher paying and in a more exciting part of the country, but didn't provide him with the chance to **grow his base of knowledge** and find a strong career pathway for himself.

Key questions to analyze before position acceptance:

One of our truly incredible graduates who has worked for over a decade for a top financial services company put together eight key questions that he feels every job seeker should try and answer before they decide on any job offer:

1) Is the company expected to grow or is the industry in trouble?
2) Will the company afford you the opportunity to be recognized for who you are and what you do?
3) What is the company culture and do you match it?
4) Does the industry interest you or challenge you?
5) Is the initial work assignment/location in a desirable area?
6) Will the position provide you with opportunities to accomplish something notable?
7) Does the company have a set advancement path or has a schedule been explained to you?
8) Does my job allow me enough flexibility to live a relatively normal life?

Sometimes the position isn't for you and it is OK to leave:

One of our students did not have a clear enough perspective on the nature of the actual position she had accepted. She did not fully realize, although she had been told, that there was a substantial amount of fieldwork in the retail support position for which she was hired. Mind you, the position paid very well, and the opportunities down the path were substantial, but the repetition was too much for this particular student and she knew she could not put her heart into it. She politely tendered her resignation after about one month on the job. Our unemployed very-recent graduate turned back to another company that had made her an offer which she had turned down. This major medical company didn't have anything at that exact moment, but promised her that they would keep her information on file and get back to her if they found something that fit her profile and interests. She also went back to a number of other companies that had expressed some interest in her. Within one year she was in a very important overseas assignment. Keep your network current and strong!

Another one of our students took a career-path position with a major high-end retailer. He had been told that there was a clear path to management and had even been given an aggressive and official timetable that a hard-working manager could expect to follow in terms of rising within the organization. After he had been with the company about six months, the company experienced some financial problems and he was called in and told by his manager that the "game plan had changed." What he once thought would be a year or so before his first promotion had suddenly shifted to two or three years before the first major promotion. For our student, that game change was not going to work at all. While still employed, our student reached out to his professors and students he knew who were with top-flight companies and changed jobs for a better career path position. Today he works at the Pacific Northwest headquarters of a major retailer, with a marketing position that is much more exciting and has greater opportunity for advancement than the company he left.

Another of our students had been with a major distributor for about eight months, had totally mastered his job, was well known and well-liked by his retail customers, but was looking at another 16 months before he would have an opportunity to either expand his territory or be promoted. So, while employed, the student started an extensive job search, repeating what he had done his senior year in college. By the time he found new employment, he had served with the first company for about ten months. When asked why he was leaving, he was able to say, "I liked the company and my manager, but to wait another 14 months to expand my territory or be promoted wasn't going to work for me. I have much more energy than that." Today he works for a Fortune 100 software supplier.

While we don't recommend changing positions until you have **at least one year** of experience on the first job, it is possible to do so. Note: it will probably be an advantage to search within the same industry as your current position. Whatever you do, don't burn any bridges with the management you are leaving, as you may want a recommendation from your employer. Be sure to part from the company as tactfully and professionally as possible. Look your supervisor in the eye and tell them why you quit, and also submit a short letter to your company's human resources representative, as you want to make sure that your reasons for leaving are on file.

Salary Package and Negotiation

Your future earnings potential depends greatly on your starting salary and though it may be your first job, all future salaries will be based on your first negotiated position. Salary negotiation *may* be a sensitive subject for students who are simply happy to land a first job. However, it is a very important step in the acceptance process. Depending on the industry and the location, typical starting salaries will range from forty to seventy-five thousand. When the company extends the offer there may be room to negotiate. Go back and talk to your professors and outside mentors who will provide guidance.

Once you receive the offer, look online on glassdoor.com for the company page and see where their offer falls on the pay scale. Glassdoor.com gives you insight to the ranges of most salaries in the professional world. Additionally, look at industry competitors to see the salary ranges for similar job descriptions. If you decide you are in a position to negotiate starting salary, you must do so with caution. Before you reach out and request a salary increase, make sure that you have a valid argument and the request will be constructive, even if you aren't granted the starting raise.

A professional approach to initiate a salary negotiation:

The negotiation is best over the phone if it can't be done in-person – don't negotiate over email! To approach the conversation professionally, we recommend you preface the discussion with the following introduction: "I am really pleased with my offer. I think it is very fair and you are definitely my first choice of a company at which to start my career. I am wondering though, do you have any flexibility on X?" First, of course, state that you are very honored and happy to have been extended an offer and look forward to being able to work with this company. You **shouldn't directly bring up other offers** that you may have received. You don't need to state any reasons for this request, unless they ask you for some justification. If you have received an offer from a big corporation, often your human resources point of contact won't be able to directly do the negotiating, but will pass on any requests. The goal is to be able to negotiate a raise without irritating the administration and while continuing to show your appreciation for the initial offer.

If you're going to request a raise, and you feel there is justification for that request, structure your argument politely, but be strong and listen to what the other party has to say. Even if you are not granted the salary increase, they will remember your request and proposal when it comes time for raises. That said, be cautious not to push too hard if they have a no-negotiation policy.

Other forms of compensation:
The salary negotiation is only one component of your potential total compensation. Our students regularly receive relocation and hiring bonuses and both of these are negotiable, some have even received stock options and others have been placed from their first day of employment into company profit-sharing plans.

Stock options are a situation where the hiring company gives you X shares of stock at a particular price. But there is always a vesting date - a date when you can exercise the option to first purchase and subsequently (if you so choose) sell the shares. Stock options are mostly granted at start-up to early-stage companies. It is less likely that an entry-level employee would receive options at a major organization.

A **relocation bonus** is a payment to help you move to your assigned location and get settled in. A relocation bonus is taxable as earned income, but you will be able to offset those taxes with the normal allowances granted to you by the Federal Tax Code for relocations. If you haven't been offered a relocation bonus there is nothing wrong with asking for one.

A **hiring bonus** is, in a sense, a way of incentivizing you to select the offering company over others. If you get such an offer you should recognize that you are in a very small and select group of graduates, as there are not many of these given out. This means the company in question really wants you to join their team.

Of the compensation categories, salary, hiring bonus and relocation expenses are those with which the company may have the greatest flexibility. Hiring bonuses may be more rigid, but it never hurts to ask. As for stock options and profit-sharing plans, it is fine to inquire if such plans are established and if you can expect the opportunity if you perform. With most large companies it is at best very difficult to negotiate 401K or equivalent retirement-type plans and it is next to impossible to negotiate health plans. However, if you are speaking with a smaller family-owned company there may be some flexibility, depending on what you feel you specifically need.

Insider Tip: After several rounds of phone interviews, one of our students was flown to a major Pacific Northwest Corporation, where he made a great impression. The next day he received the offer letter. There was a very fair salary and a generous hiring bonus. But, there was nothing about relocation. The student asked the human resources manager about the absence of any relocation package, and was prepared to accept that there wasn't anything, but he thought he should ask anyway. To his surprise, the human resources manager said, "Oh, did we leave that out? Normally we offer $10,000. I will send you an amended version!" We will never know whether leaving out the relocation was an error or a practice, but we do know that the student got the whole package because he asked politely.

Insider Tip: Even if you hear the words, "*We cannot negotiate the salary,*" consider the following. One of our students thought the salary he was offered was fair, but not exciting, but he really wanted to work for this major global company. So he asked if they would include a salary review after six months, instead of the usual one-year. The company agreed and put it in writing and he got his first review and a raise after only six months and then another review and another raise at the end of his first year.

Insider Tip: You can also negotiate the start date, but tread carefully. If you are entering into a corporate program that offers extensive training and exposure to a variety of aspects of the hiring company, be careful to be sure you aren't asking for something unrealistic. Explore with the human resources manager whatever your need for an adjusted start date might be. But be gentle and don't expect the more highly structured programs to have much flexibility here because they have to introduce you into their training cycle on very specific dates.

Insider Tip: Sometimes you have to negotiate softly but clearly. We had a student take a position with a major diversified global conglomerate. The position he was offered was one in U.S. operations. He talked to the hiring manager about the fact that he wanted ultimately to get back to Europe but that he was willing to start in the U.S.A. In his interview with the company's group president he also mentioned this desire. Everyone was positive and two key people said, "Well, do a good job at this first assignment and we will try to get you back to Europe after a year and a half." This was purely a verbal statement. Our student took the position and the hiring manager had him working from the start throughout the U.S., Canada and Mexico. At each employment evaluation review session our student made a point of reminding the interviewers of his interest in returning to Europe and his fluency in a major European language. Two years passed with no visible movement on his desire to relocate although he had shared his desire politely and clearly in writing and verbally on several occasions. He was just starting to consider changing companies when suddenly his supervisor gave him an offer to take on major responsibilities in Europe. He is in Europe today and has been frequently promoted, and is now running operations in two major countries.

The moral of this story is twofold. First, you can't expect to get all commitments in writing when you are hired, as wise managers are not going to make commitments that they may discover they cannot deliver. However, if you see something you really want down the road, you want to make sure that the hiring manager and your immediate supervisors know your desires from the beginning.

How to turn down an offer:

Over the past six months you have been searching for opportunities, and now, finally, you are in the driver's seat. With potentially multiple offers in hand, you need to professionally turn down an offer with grace and appreciation. How to do this?

In your email, it is important to show appreciation, explain that you have decided to go in another direction, and would like to stay connected with the company going forward. If you have had contact with more than one person at the company, be sure to write them a personalized explanation as well. People like to be recognized and be "in the loop" with why their company has not been selected. Additionally, people want to know what position you've accepted over their offer so explain in your email what other position you have taken.

If you've developed a close personal relationship with the representative administering the interviews or the process, or even the manager for whom you would be working, you should call and speak to them in person regarding your intention to decline the offer. This entirely depends on your perceived relationship with the human resources team and should only be done over email if you haven't developed a personal relationship with the team. If you cannot reach them over the phone after several attempts, then send an email.

A sample response email:

Dear _____,

I would sincerely like to thank you for extending me the offer to work with _____. You have a first-class organization and I am very appreciative to have had the opportunity to interact with you over the past month. However, I have decided to go in another direction and have accepted a position with _____. Over the past month I have been treated with the greatest respect and your team has made this process very exciting and enjoyable. I would like to stay in touch and wish you and Company X the best of luck in the future!

With much appreciation,

Janet Jobseeker

Turning down a job you've already accepted?

While we do not recommend continuing to apply to jobs after you've accepted an offer, sometimes you find yourself in the position of turning down an offer *after* you've accepted it, which is a much more difficult process. Once you've accepted the offer, organizations start notifying other applicants that they haven't been chosen and close the requisition. Though you **most likely** don't have a legally binding contract, you will need to be aware of the most ethical steps to quickly turning down an offer after you've accepted. Some reasons are legitimate though they may not be viewed as such at the organization. It is paramount that you do this over the phone, if you can't notify them in person. Email **will not** suffice. While doing so, it is important to understand their needs and help them through the repercussions of you turning down the position. Do so with honesty and a positive attitude, and remember, you're filling a lower-level position for the company and are relatively easily replaceable!

While we recommend only accepting an offer you really want and not shopping once you have an offer, we want to point out that in most cases companies are under no or very limited obligation to honor their offers. Additionally, we know of one renowned university's career services program that retains the right to ban students from its career placement system if they reject an offer they have already accepted.

Accepting the offer!

When you choose to accept an offer, there will be a number of methods to officially accept, varying from company to company. It is important to personally contact each person you have worked with through the application and let them know that you have received an offer and that you appreciate their individual help in your application process. Considering that these will now be your coworkers, it is important to get off on the right foot and explain your appreciation by sharing how they influenced your decision.

Social media and Background checks:
Upon accepting a full-time position, depending on the size of the organization, you will receive a comprehensive background check, social media check (companies will check all social media platforms), drug test and sometimes a credit check. The background check will occur simultaneously as the offer is given, while the drug test will require you to go to a testing center after your acceptance of the offer. In addition to background checks and drug tests, employers will run a credit report and check into any arrests. Arrests, including DUIs, are reasons to immediately dismiss an applicant from a position. If you have arrests on your record, be sure to bring this up to any mentors or advocates before you request a recommendation for a position.

Section V Summary:
Though receiving that first offer will certainly provide you some relief, a portion of your work has just begun after you accept the position. Having just gone through an arduous process, you deserve at least a short break, but you are still required to complete important actions before you can rest with a full-time offer. Closing the offer, declining any other outstanding offers, and thanking all those who have helped you are all important steps and deserve serious effort. Additionally, it is suggested to send these contacts and mentors an "update and hello" email after one year in

your current position to let them know your progress.

Get to Work Conclusion

Our goal with this text is to help students increase their odds for success in the job-search process. We walked you through the internship- and career-search process, starting with ways to build your resume as a freshman all the way through negotiating your starting salary in your senior year. *Get to Work* is designed to give you a step-by-step manual for this seemingly daunting process – we hope it did just that. We wish you the best of luck in the search and please contact us with any questions or comments regarding the material, or if you have any specific questions during your personal career search and application process – our email address is contactgettowork@gmail.com. Good luck and thank you for reading!

Abridged Action Summary

This checklist is established to give students a quick overview of each necessary step in the job search process. If you haven't read the preceding sections, this outline is designed to provide you with brief overview of the fundamental steps, allowing you to revisit any area of question.

Pre-Application:

- Understanding yourself:
  - o What are your strengths?
  - o What are your interests?
  - o What are your goals?

Strengths:	Weaknesses	Interests:

Two Year Goals:	Five Year Goals:	Ten Year Goals:

- Identify industries of interest
  - What are your interests? Sports? Aviation? Cars? Food? Media? Fashion? Social Networking? Mobile technology?

  _____
  _____
  _____

- Identify functional paths of interest
  - What are your target functional paths? Accounting? Sales? General management?

  _____
  _____
  _____

- Gathering sources for developing external contacts
  - Follow companies and join groups on LinkedIn

- o Attend meet-ups/local conferences of your interest
- o Join a young professionals community

- Who are your internal contacts?
  - o Family friends
    1. _____
    2. _____
    3. _____
  - o Professors
    1. _____
    2. _____
    3. _____
  - o Coaches/Mentors
    1. _____
    2. _____
    3. _____
  - o Alumni
    1. _____
    2. _____
    3. _____

- Gather your best work and official transcripts

- Join on-campus groups/associations/classes to get an insight to the industry and add to your resume

The Application:

- Visit online databases and create a list of companies of interest

- o Find points of contact and their email addresses/phone numbers

- Set out strategy for your application process
  - o **Step 1:** Filter through company websites to find points of contacts and HR emails/links
  - o **Step 2:** Read and thoroughly the job description
  - o **Step 3:** Learn how to address the requirements you don't meet
  - o **Step 4:** Identify any tripwires or focus words in their resume filters
  - o **Step 5:** Apply to the group of pre-selected companies
  - o **Step 6:** Send follow-up emails to both the HR department and internal points of contact three days later

Post Application/Pre-Interview:

- Continue to research your company by reading pre-interview websites such as glassdoor.com to understand the general theme of the interview

- Prepare your situational questions and answers
  - o Cover all major requisition themes: i.e. leadership, teamwork, etc.

- Prepare your "10 stories" mentioned in Section III
  - Outline your STAR format responses to situational questions
  - Diversify your responses
    - Find additional stories to convey central themes if you find yourself relying too heavily on one or two experiences

- Write out your notes for the interview introduction and closure
  - Prepare intro "Tell me a little about yourself" and "walk me through your resume"
  - Prepare your closing

- Prepare three to five questions to ask the interviewer

- If you know who will be interviewing you, research the individual and know their background. Demonstrate that you've done your homework in the interview

- Read through the companies 10-K, 10-Q, specifically the MD&A Section

- Read through industry research papers online and formulate thoughts to explain where the company is headed due to its macro environment.

- Follow the companies you've applied to on Google News

- Follow industry news journals and key financial newspapers

Day of interview:
- Repeat your opening "About yourself" and "closing pitch" in a mirror
- Bring six resumes on nice paper, a notebook and a pen
- Dress appropriately
- Arrive at least 30 minutes early
- After the interview, ask to sit with someone in your role (if applicable/possible)
- Take down any names you hear
- Tell them you want the job!
- **Smile**!

After the interview
- Send follow-up thank you emails
- Thank **all** contacts who helped you with the interview process
- Reach out to anyone you've met that day with a "thank you" note
- Continue to study the industry and follow the company.
- Practice your computer and Excel skills

THE END

80816446R00119